WHEN ELIJAH KNOCKS
A Religious Response To Homelessness

According to Jewish tradition, Elijah the prophet, an advocate of the poor, was himself homeless. Before he died, he announced that he would return once in every generation disguised as a poor, oppressed person, knocking at the doors of Jewish homes. How Elijah was treated would determine whether humanity was ready to enter the Messianic age.

Behrman House Publishers

WHEN ELIJAH KNOCKS

◆─────────────────────◆

A RELIGIOUS RESPONSE TO HOMELESSNESS

Rabbi Charles A. Kroloff

Project editor: Adam Bengal
Designer: Susan Lampton

© Copyright 1992, Rabbi Charles A. Kroloff

Published by Behrman House, Inc.
235 Watchung Ave.
West Orange, NJ 07052
(800) 221-2755

92 93 94 95

Library of Congress Cataloging-in-Publication Data

Kroloff, Charles A.
    When Elijah knocks : a religious response to homelessness / by
Charles A. Kroloff.
176 p.
    Includes bibliographical references and index.
    ISBN 0-87441-516-0
    1. Homelessness – United States. 2. Voluntarism – United States.
3. Homelessness – Religious aspects.   I. Title.
HV4505.K76   1992
363.5′575′0973 – dc20   92-508
                                                           CIP

To the Homeless
Men, Women and Children
of Our Land

CONTENTS

ACKNOWLEDGEMENTS

◆ ─────────────────────────────────────── ◆

*T*hroughout the United States, there are tens of thousands of citizens working as professionals and volunteers to deal with the growing problem of homelessness. They can be found in nearly every town and city, in government and not-for-profit agencies, in corporations and universities, in churches, synagogues, and mosques, in shelters and on the streets.

During my research for this book, I have been privileged to meet some rare human beings. At enormous personal sacrifice, they have dedicated their lives to helping the millions of men, women, and children who live under conditions that should be intolerable in a civilized country. Each has a dozen stories of failure and success, of despair and hope. They do not give up. They have shared with me their vision and enabled me to meet the homeless of our land.

I express my profound appreciation to Pincus Berger, Rabbi Gary Bretton-Granatoor, Sister Alice Callaghan, Terry Carillio, Peggy Comfrey, Patrick Conover, Bob Davis, Father Bill Doulos, Clare Doyle, Peter Fine, Ruth Flower, Richelle Friedman, Dan Hardy, Pat Irish, Rabbi Richard Jacobs, Rabbi Lynne Landsberg, Alexia Kelley, Randi Locke, Sister Jane McKenzie, Caroline Miller, Stephen Moses, Karen Olson, Sara Peller, Rabbi Sanford Ragins, Ed Rehfeld, Toni Reinis, Rabbi David Saperstein, Jerald Scott, Tom Shellabarger, Fred Siegel, Marlene Singer, Laura Spitzer, Rhoda Stauffer, Glenn Stein, Rev. John F. Steinbruck, Rabbi Lennard Thal, Al Vorspan, Rev. John Wightman, Robert Zdenek, and so many others who shared their work and insights with me.

The demands of congregational life make it nearly impossible to find extended blocks of uninterrupted time in which to write. I am grateful to the members of my synagogue, Temple

Emanu-El of Westfield, New Jersey, who afforded me a Sabattical leave during which *When Elijah Knocks* was written. My associate, Rabbi Marc Disick, and the Temple president, Robert Koppel, were particularly helpful. My administrative assistant, Laura Nadel, my secretary, Corinne Bernstein, and the entire staff of Temple Emanu-El contributed to this effort.

The idea for this book was born in the sensitive soul of Adam Bengal, my editor and friend. Adam lovingly and creatively nurtured this project at every stage along the way. He and Jacob Behrman frequently had more confidence in me than I dared to expect. Kim Fryer has edited the text superbly and Barbara Koppel has written the index.

My wife, Terry, an editor in her own right, not only offered a critique which consistently sharpened the focus, but she has encouraged me to undertake and complete this project. Without her patience and support, it would not have seen the light of day. Each of our children, Micah, Donna, Noah, Sarah and Roger, offered helpful suggestions.

I dedicate this book to the homeless of our land. And I pray that our grandson Adam will grow up in a nation where our most vulnerable citizens will never have to spend a single night on the streets or in the shelters of America.

Charles A. Kroloff

Westfield, New Jersey
May 15, 1992

The author gratefully acknowledges the following:

Bill Doulos, Director, Church and Temple Housing Corporation. Selection reprinted with permission.

Family Circle, Feb. 20, 1990; "Women Who Make a Difference," by Steven Kaplan. Reprinted with permission.

Kushner, Rabbi Harold S.: From *Who Needs God?* Summit Books, Simon & Schuster, Inc. Reprinted with permission.

"Man in the Mirror," words and music by Glen Ballard and Siedah Garrett. © Copyright 1987 by MCA Music Publishing, a division of MCA Inc., Aerostation Corporation and Yellowbrick Road Music. Rights of Aerostation Corporation administered by MCA Music Publishing, a division of MCA Inc., New York, NY, 10019. Used by permission. All rights reserved.

The New York Times, Nov. 23, 1989; "Fund for the Neediest Helps Man Leave Homelessness Behind," by Nadine Brozan. Reprinted with permission.

The New York Times, Mar. 12, 1990; "Homeless, They Build for Peers," by Alan Finder. Reprinted with permission.

The New York Times, Mar. 27, 1990; "Sensitivity Ebbs and Often Flows, In Homeless Plan," by Michael Winerip. Reprinted with permission.

The New York Times, May 21, 1990; "Children Striving to Cope with the Homeless," by Dennis Hevesi. Reprinted with permission.

Steinbruck, Rev. John; selection from "The Shalom Vision for Housing." Reprinted with permission.

Gerald Winterlin. Selection reprinted with permission.

PART ONE

Who are the Homeless?

1
WHO ARE THE HOMELESS?

◆───────────────────────────────◆

*T*he homeless have always been among us. Their numbers had never been great, however, except during the days of the Great Depression. And rarely, if ever, did they include a family who once lived next door or an employee at a fashionable department store. The homeless were generally thought of as tramps and hoboes—perpetual transients. Many were alcoholics who lived in single-room occupancy hotels (SROs) or in missions operated by the Salvation Army or inner-city churches.

All that has changed.

Today's homeless have multiplied in number and include men, women and children. A good number, such as elderly people on fixed incomes, do not fit the traditional image of homeless folk. But the fact is that a senior citizen who receives $450 a month in benefits and pays $350 for rent cannot survive in most U.S. cities.

Many Americans prefer to think of the homeless as former mental patients, drug-abusers or ne'er-do-wells. That gives us an excuse not to deal with homeless people or their problems.

"They are perpetual social problems," we say. "They've always been with us and they always will be." We try not to think of the homeless as a former next-door neighbor and are not as troubled if we picture them as belonging in an institution.

That is why we do not like to hear the truth: many Americans are working full-time and are still homeless. According to the United States Conference of Mayors, one out of four homeless persons is *employed* full- or part-time. The arithmetic is simple and frightening: a single person who works forty hours a week at the 1992 Federal minimum wage of $4.25 per hour would gross about $700 a month, take home little less than $600 – and be a prime candidate for homelessness.

I meet such people at the shelter run by my synagogue in Westfield, New Jersey. Two neatly dressed sisters in their thirties arrived one evening seeking overnight housing. After they were assigned a room and had enjoyed dinner, I spoke with one of them about her situation and her hopes for the future.

She was employed full-time as a salesclerk at Bloomingdale's; her sister was seeking a job. Two rent increases in one year had consumed their modest savings and caused them to fall behind in their rent. Consequently, they were evicted from their home. By using the Temple's hospitality program instead of paying for temporary housing such as a motel room, they hoped to save $2100 – enough for first and last months' rent and a security deposit on a $600-a-month dwelling.

In such diverse cities as Denver, Los Angeles, Nashville, Phoenix and Alexandria, Virginia, over thirty percent of the homeless are employed.[1] Homeless people are not necessarily unwilling to do a good day's work. Many simply cannot find jobs which will pay enough to cover food, clothing, utilities and *especially* rent.

Disabled Veterans
and Children

The numbers of homeless have increased as our national problems have proliferated. And each problem seems to produce a new population of homeless people.

One-quarter of the homeless are veterans, mostly from the Vietnam war. Do you remember Ron Kovic's story in the film *Born on the Fourth of July*? Recall how desperate and alone the veterans became and how easy it was for them to end up discouraged and abandoned on our nation's streets. Like Ron from Massapequa, New York, a homeless person can be the boy or girl next door.

Thirty-two thousand people with AIDS and their dependents were homeless in 1989, and over 100,000 AIDS-related victims are projected to join their ranks by 1995.[2] Undocumented immigrants are also becoming homeless in growing numbers.

Blacks and other minorities are over-represented among the homeless, while whites and Asians are under-represented. The majority of homeless people are male, with single men constituting about two-thirds of the total population. The elderly are disproportionately less than other minorities, perhaps because Medicare and other senior-oriented programs provide a safety net.

More and More
Homeless Children

One out of every four homeless people is a child, a new tragedy in America. The fastest-growing group of the homeless in the United States has been families with children, a category that has nearly doubled from 1984 to 1989.

Agencies in Los Angeles report that in 1989 they started to

see homeless children for the first time at missions in the downtown skid row area, which have traditionally served only single men.[3] California's Department of Social Services estimates that *during the course of a year* 50,000 children are homeless in Los Angeles and 200,000 in the state.

Based on the numbers served by shelters, the National Coalition for the Homeless reckons that *on any given night* a quarter of a million youths are homeless in the nation.[4]

I was shocked to learn that in Washington, D.C., a soup line opened for destitute children who were under the age of twelve. Known as Martha's Table, within three weeks the soup line was serving thirty children a day. One of the first guests was a three-year-old boy who was "escorting" a seventeen-month-old child.[5]

Many homeless children are unaccompanied by adults. They may be runaways who left home because there is no money for food or because one or both of their parents are in emotional turmoil or because they are victims of rape, incest or other forms of domestic and street violence.

Some are "throwaway" children whose parents tell them to leave home or runaways who are not allowed to return.[6] Most of us would find it difficult to imagine a parent telling a sixteen-year-old child that he/she must leave home and never return. But that scene is repeated again and again every day in the cities of America.

Unaccompanied youths account for ten percent or more of the homeless population in Denver, Los Angeles, New Orleans, San Francisco and Santa Monica. They have a difficult time getting into shelters, many of which are afraid to assume liability and will not accept teenagers fifteen to eighteen years of age.[7] Chicago offers only thirty emergency beds for 10,000 homeless youth – so most end up spending nights on the street, under bridges and in public parks.

Homeless children are part of a larger national tragedy. According to the National Commission on Children, the poorest age group in the United States is children, with one child in five living below the poverty line. As a result, the Commission predicted that "many of today's children will reach adulthood unhealthy, illiterate and unemployable." Said Dr. T. Berry Brazelton, Professor of Pediatrics at Harvard, "We know these kids are going to cost us billions. . . . They're going to be the terrorists of the future."[8]

These children become easy targets for pimps, drug dealers and molesters. Ironically, those who ran away from sexual abuse and violence at home frequently suffer that same abuse on the streets.

An Eight-Year-Old's View of the Homeless	*Well, time to go begging on the street. Usually no one gives me anything, but it's worth a try anyway. Yesterday I didn't get anything because I was in a bad mood, yelling out all these bad words for no reason. See, no one understands that when you're homeless you have so many trapped emotions inside that you just explode.*[9]
	Kate Wilson

When it comes to taking care of children, our country has a horrendous record, ranking with Malaysia – far below most Western countries. Children have no lobby in Washington, D.C.: they are voiceless and helpless. Is it any wonder that their plight has *never* been a major concern of any presidential candidate?

Families in all walks of life are under intense pressure today. For homeless families, the pressure is unbearable. If a family becomes homeless in Chicago, Cleveland, New Orleans, Phoenix or Portland, it is forced to break up in order to be accommodated in emergency shelters.[10] If a man has a female child or a woman has boys over twelve, family shelters will not handle them.

The lack of shelter facilities for families has led to conditions that are intolerable for this nation: Portland, Oregon, turns away 220 homeless families every month. Los Angeles's shelters reject 1,800 family members *each day*! Little wonder: in 1986, Los Angeles had one shelter bed for every fifteen needed. In Phoenix, seventy percent of the requests for emergency shelter went unmet during 1989. Cleveland authorities report that the county will house a family in a hotel only "if the temperature is below 32 degrees. Otherwise, the family goes without."[11]

What happens when families and unaccompanied youth cannot be accommodated? Seattle officials report, "Those who cannot be served often sleep on the streets. Youths may double up or prostitute themselves in order to secure a place."[12]

"Any society has to be judged by how it cares for those who are weakest." Plato said that 3,000 years ago about the elderly. In 1988, the United States Catholic Conference reminded us that "we shall be judged by our response to 'the least among us' . . . the quality of justice is best measured by how the poor and most vulnerable are faring."[13]

By those standards, we should hang our heads in shame.

◆ *In a sense, the homeless are like the canaries used by nineteenth century miners to detect dangerous gases deep in the mines: they warn us that something is seriously wrong in our*
◆ *society.*[14]

Aren't Most Homeless Mentally Ill and Drug Abusers?

Most of us would like to avoid dealing with the problem of homelessness. One way is to argue that most homeless people are former mental patients who have been deinstitutionalized. Where does that idea come from? In the 1960s and 1970s mental institutions were viewed as merely "warehousing" many patients. With the advent of new antipsychotic drugs, as many as 366,000 patients were released on the assumption that they would do as well outside the facility as within. Some critics now claim that if these former patients were readmitted, homelessness would virtually disappear.

Nothing could be further from the truth. Most homeless are not mentally ill. True, many are emotionally disturbed and suffer from personality disorders. However, if they receive medication, are removed from the street and taken care of, they often can be restored to lives of dignity, if not minimal self-sufficiency.

Most of the emotionally disturbed have a sense of reality that enables them to function at a modest level within society. Dysfunction is often the *result* of being homeless, not its *cause*. Wouldn't most of us have a skewed sense of reality if we spent night after night on the streets or in a shelter?

A study of 500 homeless people in Baltimore revealed that while more than half needed outpatient psychiatric treatment, only fifteen percent required short-term inpatient psychiatric care and a mere *one percent* were candidates for long-term hospitalization.[15] Other studies suggest that in our major cities approximately twenty-five percent of the homeless suffer from mental illness. It is a large segment, of which some need institutionalization, but it is not the bulk of the homeless.

In cities where a large proportion of the homeless are children under fourteen, we have even less of a basis to assume that most of the homeless are former mental patients. These children were not even born when mental patients were deinstitutionalized. Nor is it likely that the children's parents, who are usually under thirty, were mental patients during their teens.[16]

On the Thursday after Christmas in 1990, 3,853 families—

more than 12,000 people—stayed at shelters operated by the city of New York. The number of single men and women sheltered by the city at the same time was 9,950. On that snowy night, the city was accommodating more families than singles.[17]

What about the notion that the homeless are heavy drug users? Research suggests that one in three of the homeless is a substance abuser, although the Baltimore study revealed lower figures—twenty percent of homeless men and seventeen percent of the women.[18]

Why do we rush to brand the homeless as substance abusers? I believe we do so in order to shift responsibility from us to them. It is easier to blame homeless addicts or alcoholics for getting themselves into their predicament than it is to label a child of ten "guilty" for *causing* his or her own homelessness.

Many Homeless
Live on the Margins

Yes, some of the homeless *are* substances abusers. But many are victims who have been living on the margins of society for years until something occurs—such as the loss of a job, hospitalization, the death of a supportive parent or a physical disability—that pushes them over the edge into homelessness.

Consider Joe S. of Brooklyn, who had been in and out of drug treatment programs. He had been just getting by on his wage as a warehouse porter and with a little help from a relative until two major changes occurred within a few months. The company for which he worked moved its Brooklyn warehouse to South Carolina and Joe's thoughtful relative retired on drastically reduced income and could no longer assist him. Finding himself on the unemployment line, Joe dropped out of drug treatment and soon became homeless.

In more ways than not, the homeless are like us. While some

inhabit streets, parks, tunnels and shanties under bridges, many have just been evicted from a room, apartment or small home. Often they have been living doubled or tripled up with family or friends and finally were asked to leave. Ten to twenty million families live doubled or tripled up in the United States, with half a million in New York state alone.[19]

Many homeless people have completed high school; some have attended college and even graduate school. They have children, brothers, sisters and parents. Some go to church or synagogue. Not only can they be found in cities, but also in small towns, rural areas and, yes, our affluent suburbs.

How Many Homeless?
A Census Taker's Challenge

Estimates of the homeless *on any given night* in the United States range from 600,000 by a research institute to three million by an advocacy group. The number who are homeless for *at least one night during the year* is probably well in excess of three million.

California officials estimate 150,000 homeless in that state alone. In New York state, the figure approaches 100,000, while even a sparsely populated state like Colorado reports 15,000-20,000. Most regional attempts to estimate the number of homeless yield figures of 0.7 to 1.1 percent of a community's population.[20] If these calculations can be accurately applied to the nation as a whole, homeless people across the United States may number in excess of two million.

This does not account for the hidden homeless—millions more who are one crisis away from homelessness. They may be doubled or tripled up in housing or forty-eight hours from eviction or about to leave a hospital with nowhere to go.

On March 20, 1990, the U.S. Census Bureau attempted to count the homeless. Yvette Black, homeless for eight years and living in a Los Angeles mission, said, "It felt good to be counted.

Maybe something good will happen; now, maybe they'll recognize us." In an Albuquerque shelter, Mitchell Birdshead, 35, echoed Ms. Black: "This is the first time we've ever had anybody come out and ask us stuff, like we mattered."[21]

Estimates of Albuquerque's homeless range from 1,200 (city officials) to 4,000 (homeless advocates). With less than one-third sleeping in shelters, assessments of the number of homeless who were not counted ranged as high as seventy percent. At the city's largest day shelter, St. Martin's, seventeen of the forty-five homeless men and women who showed up for breakfast the day after the tally said they had not been included in the census.[22]

At Miami's biggest shelter, Camillaus House, 1,120 meals were served on census night, but only 350 people filled out the forms. A Baltimore official claimed that at least twenty percent of the homeless shelters were missed by the census takers.[23] A Los Angeles study estimates that fifty-nine to seventy percent of that city's homeless were not counted.[24]

> ◆ *Carmen M. Luna, a thirty-nine-year-old widow and mother of two teenagers, said that her apprehensions about assisting with the New York homeless census vanished as compassion overtook her. "It was educational, it was sad, it was a lot of emotions rolled into one," she said. "I've always felt for them, but now that I've seen them, I'm more aware of how we really, really have to do something to try to get these people a*
> ◆ *home."[25]*

James Wright, a sociologist, observed about the homeless: "In many respects the advocacy community is correct in saying these people are intrinsically uncountable. They have too many good ways of avoiding detection and too many good reasons for wanting to avoid detection."[26]

Why do people who live on the edge of homelessness fear being counted? A Bronx man in his sixties shares a one-bedroom government-subsidized building with three relatives – his son, his daughter-in-law and their nine-month-old baby – without the knowledge of the landlord or the welfare office. He fears that if the "sharing" is disclosed, his rent will rise or he will lose his $278 in public assistance. No census forms will be returned from that "at risk" household.[27]

Attempts to count the homeless always end in failure – and so do attempts to blot them from our consciousness. We cannot escape from the blatant reality that homelessness is growing: the annual growth rate was estimated at eighteen percent in 1988-1989 by the Partnership for the Homeless – and higher according to other studies.[28]

Every one of us needs to feel that we matter, that we count in someone else's reckoning, that we count in God's scheme of things. All the more so with the homeless. They especially need to feel important to someone, that they are not totally alone in this world, that people care, that God cares.

But too many of us do not care because we have accepted the prevailing myths about homelessness. The purpose of this chapter is to help us understand the facts about the homeless so we can become strong advocates on their behalf. Let's continue to educate – or perhaps reeducate – ourselves by looking at some of the prevailing myths concerning the homeless.

2
DISPELLING
THE MYTHS

◆————————————————————————————◆

We have created unreal and unfair myths about the home-less, which have led many of us to write these people off. Here are common ideas concerning the homeless and some facts that can help us gain a new perspective:

Some people want to be homeless.

> FACT: Less than six percent of the homeless are in that situation by choice.[1]

The homeless are to blame for being homeless.

> FACT: One-quarter of all homeless are children. Many others are traumatized Vietnam veterans. Still others are victims of child abuse or of street or domestic violence. Are they to blame? Most homeless people are the *victims*, not the causes, of a system that does not protect its most vulnerable members.

The homeless don't work.

> FACT: Many homeless people are among the working poor. A person working forty hours a week at the 1992 minimum wage of $4.25 per hour cannot earn enough to lift a family of three out of poverty or pay inner-city rent.

Most of the homeless are mentally ill persons who have been released from mental institutions.

> FACT: About twenty-five percent of the homeless in most cities are mentally ill. As few as one percent may require long-term hospitalization.

All homeless people are poor. The myths we have about the poor affect how we feel about the homeless. As a result of these myths, we stereotype the poor and homeless, which is counterproductive and prevents us from relating to them as the human beings they are.

Most poor people are black and most black people are poor.

> FACT: Neither is true. Most poor Americans are white, not black. Since the poverty rate for blacks (thirty-four percent) is about three times that for whites, many think that poverty in the United States is largely a black problem. About one-third of all blacks are poor, but two-thirds are not. Poverty is growing more rapidly among whites than blacks: in 1978-1984, the number of whites in poverty grew by forty-one percent as compared to a twenty-five percent growth for blacks. Poverty and homelessness are problems for *all* Americans.[2]

The poor will always be with us.

FACT: Evidence indicates that we can reduce poverty. The poverty rate dropped from thirty percent in 1950 to eleven percent in 1973. It has now risen to fourteen percent. Nor is poverty necessarily a *permanent* condition. A study that tracked 5,000 families found nearly one-fourth remained poor for one or more years, but only 2.6 percent were poor for eight or more years.[3]

Most people in poverty live in inner-city ghettos.

FACT: Only fourteen percent of the nation's poor live in what the Census Bureau calls "poverty areas" of our central cities. Twenty-two percent of all poor families live in the central cities, but outside of poverty areas. Thirty-nine percent of the poor live in nonmetropolitan areas.[4]

What about low-income housing? How great is the shortage and what should be the role of government in meeting that need? Here are some of the myths that abound:

No shortage of housing exists in North America.

FACT: A 1986 study found that the number of citizens living under the poverty level *increased* by thirty-six percent over six years while the number of affordable housing units *decreased* by thirty percent. Vacancy rates in New York, San Francisco and Boston averaged one to two percent in the late eighties. (Five percent is normal.)[5]

17

Housing is a problem that only the government can solve.

> FACT: Community-based organizations, with
> government support, have produced
> hundreds of thousands of low-income
> units in recent years. They have also
> encouraged economic and social stability
> in neighborhoods.

Housing is a problem that we can solve by ourselves.

> FACT: Although community-based groups
> have made an impact, they can never do
> the job alone. The number of homeless is
> growing faster than the number of units
> these groups can create. Without strong
> government support, the availability of
> affordable housing cannot keep pace
> with the already tragic level of homeless-
> ness, let alone overtake it.

*The federal government has been pouring money into low-income housing
for decades and it has not worked.*

> FACT: To some extent, low-income housing
> programs have worked. Since Congress
> set broad housing goals in 1949, millions
> of substandard slums have been elimi-
> nated. The quality of housing has im-
> proved, and the home ownership rate in
> the United States is one of the highest in
> the world – largely because of the gov-
> ernment. But spending has remained at
> the same one percent of the federal bud-
> get. Bad things are happening because
> government is not spending enough.[6]

18

Only the poor receive government subsidies for housing.

> FACT: Mitch Snyder once addressed an affluent group and asked: "Would everyone who lives in federally-subsidized housing please raise your hands." No one did. Then he asked: "How many are home-owners?" All raised their hands. The government subsidizes homeowners to the tune of $50 billion annually through tax deductions. Every homeowner present was government-subsidized and didn't know it.

Transitional and low-income housing create problems of crime and drugs in the neighborhood.

> FACT: When transitional and low-income housing is combined with tenant em-powerment and support from com-munity- based groups and religious insti-tutions, crime and drugs actually decrease.

If we live in middle-class suburbs or in higher-income sections of our cities, we deceive ourselves into believing that the problem is out of our area. Here is what some people be-lieve. . . .

If a church of synagogue is not in an urban area and few homeless are nearby, little exists that those institutions can do.

> FACT: Churches and synagogues are sheltering and feeding thousands who are trans-ported from nearby urban areas. These institutions are also the pillars of community-based groups that build or

rehabilitate tens of thousands of housing units. The religious community's potential as advocates for greater government support is unlimited.

Putting shelters in synagogues and churches is a high-risk operation.

FACT: Occasional reports of petty theft are received from shelters. On the other hand, reports of violence or other serious crimes are almost nonexistent.

Perhaps the most pernicious myth of all is the one that claims that. . .

People do not care about the homeless.

The FACT is that public opinion polls reveal that the American people consider homelessness a top priority and are willing to pay more taxes to solve the problem.

Americans are mostly a compassionate people, and we are troubled by the enormous gaps between rich and poor in our land. Many of us do not sleep easily knowing that hundreds of thousands of men, women *and children* are sleeping on grates, under bridges and in doorways. Many of us do not enjoy our meals knowing that vast numbers of Americans are going hungry.

The following chapter will address the myth that the homeless are mostly bums. In my research for this book, I have met many homeless persons through personal interviews, correspondence and newspaper reports. Some of them have turned their lives around; their stories are inspiring.

3
"WE ARE NOT BUMS"

How The Homeless See Themselves

> In a southern town in 1989, after a homeless man was accused of homicide, the municipal council passed an ordinance ordering all the homeless out of town. The city commissioner declared, "When I was a child, we didn't call these people homeless; we called them bums. I don't see any reason not to still call them bums."

"There are bums that want to be bums. You can't help them people until they want to be helped. But there's a lot of people who want help." Jim Robinson was talking about himself.

Robinson lived an uneventful life on the beaches of Atlantic City until he and another homeless man were photographed sleeping in front of swimsuit-clad Miss America contestants on September 9, 1989. As police ejected forty-two-year-old Robinson and his friend from an overturned lifeboat that sheltered them, the contestants' photo session was interrupted and the two men landed on the front pages of newspapers across the country.

Before becoming homeless, Robinson had driven taxis in Atlantic City for seven years. At one point, he had used cocaine steadily for nearly a year, spending a $70,000 inheritance – sometimes at the rate of $3,000 a week. After several rehabilitation programs, an attempted suicide and ten months in a psychiatric hospital, he was released to a halfway house and soon found work as a security guard. After losing that job, he became homeless.

Robinson wasn't happy about being photographed. "I didn't want my friends to see me." A day after the photo session, his friend, Jeff Hall, was found dead of a heart attack on the beach. His death inspired Robinson to do something about his own life. "It made me a stronger person. It gave me something to do for a cause."

A week after the beach incident, Robinson moved in with a cousin and her husband, a retired New York City transit police officer. "When he called us," said the officer, "I took it as an indication that he wanted help."

Robinson soon landed a job in the mailroom of Penguin USA, a publishing firm located near his cousin's home. "It's nice to work for a change," he said. "I'm not making a lot of money, but it's fine."[1]

I have met many homeless people whose relatives will have nothing to do with them. What would you or I do if we received a call today from a friend or relative who was living in a shelter or on the street? If Jim's cousin had turned him away, where would he be?

From Homelessness to Academic Heights

What we are prepared to do for the homeless – relatives or strangers – depends a great deal on what we think of them. If we are convinced that they are human debris, we assume that they will never escape our cities' trash-heaps and any help we render is wasted effort.

But what if we believe that, like the rest of us, they have untapped resources buried within? What if we sense that there is potential that needs to be identified and nurtured? True, sometimes those resources seem so remote as to be unreachable. But at times the promise is there, waiting for the right combination of circumstances to release it. That was the case with Gerald Winterlin.

Winterlin's plunge into homelessness began as the Midwest's farm economy collapsed in the early 1980s. Employed as a laborer at a farm-equipment plant, he was laid off in May 1982. He soon lost his home and slept in the rear of his station wagon. When that broke down, he spent his nights in abandoned homes.

Frustrated by his failure to find employment, he read in the newspaper about a program that assisted dislocated workers. He applied, took a skills text and, with the help of a Federal Pell Grant, attended junior college. Two years later, he enrolled at the University of Iowa. He graduated in December 1990 at the age of forty-four with a degree in accounting and a nearly perfect grade point average of 3.966![2]

"There are a million Jerry Winterlins running around this country," he told me. Perhaps there are a million. Or maybe only 100,000. No one will ever know how many. But vast numbers of homeless men and women who are capable of gaining their high school equivalency degree, attending college and holding down a productive job do exist.

◆ *Gerald Winterlin received several scholarships as he made his way through the University of Iowa. One of them was from the Roy J. Carver*
(Cont.)

Trust, which awards stipends to people "who have overcome extreme social or psychological barriers."

Mr. Carver wanted to attended medical school, but his family had little money during the Great Depression. Instead, he studied engineering and founded Bandag, a successful tire-retreading company in Muscatine, Iowa. When he died, he left a charitable trust currently worth $137 million for the purpose of rewarding perseverance and initiative.

Other Carver scholarship winners attending schools in Iowa include a widowed mother of six in her forties, an eighteen-year-old whose plans for college were dashed when her parents lost their farm in the rural crisis of the 1980s and a thirty-year-old, hearing impaired and severely dyslexic, who is studying mechanical engineering.

◆   *Roy J. Carver has made quite a difference.*

Within Us All:
Untapped Resources

Each of us has rich untapped resources of which we are only dimly aware. Some can paint or craft things of beauty. Others have the potential to engage in competitive sports, to photograph or to write. But most of us have never taken the time or been stimulated enough to tap those hidden capabilities.

I meet many retired persons who in their later years, with leisure and maturity, have discovered natural gifts that were concealed by the pressures of making a living and raising a family. I have seen the sculptures they fashioned, the canvases they painted, the children they tutored, the gardens they tended and the histories they recorded.

So it is with many homeless people. Their talents, buried deep within, are covered by layers of neglect, self-abuse or illness. Often what is needed is the combination of a homeless person who wants to be helped and an individual who cares enough to get involved and persevere.

That combination produces incredible results. It explodes the tired stereotype that homeless people do not want to be helped. And it makes believable what Judaism and Christianity teach: that every one of us can make a difference.

Consider Albert Bishop, the son of a violinist and furniture dealer from Guyana. Bishop's future seemed bright until he was struck with a kidney disease that required him to undergo dialysis three times a week. Using his training in plumbing, carpentry, electrical work and tiling, he had spent his days off renovating a house that he had bought in the Bronx. But it was not yet habitable when he became ill.

When the disease forced him to leave his job as a security guard in 1984, Bishop became homeless. He missed the deadlines to apply for public and subsidized housing because he was hospitalized.

Once he was released from the hospital, he lived for a while with a friend whom he later discovered was on crack. Meanwhile, Bishop sought help from every agency he could contact, visited projects and wrote his congressman. As the situation reached crisis proportions at his friend's apartment, he decided to put down on paper his entire medical and housing history.

He brought that history to Catholic Charities, where Ruth Francis, a caseworker, became his advocate. For eight months, she helped him track down subsidized housing. By insisting that the agencies respond *to her*, she kept the process going even when Bishop was hospitalized.

Finding the Beautiful
Places of the City

During the whole ordeal, Bishop never lost hope and maintained his dignity and pursued his interests. "I always kept my spirits up by going to the beautiful places of the city: the library, Central Park; if I had an extra quarter, to the Metropolitan Museum of Art.

"Even when I was living in the shelters, I would get up and say, 'I think I'll have breakfast on Wall Street today.' I would get on the train and be a part of the bustle." Albert Bishop never lost sight of the beauty of life. His spirit remained strong because he kept in touch with the good things of life that did not cost a penny: the library, the park, the museum and, for a splurge, breakfast on Wall Street.

In September 1989, Bishop, who lives on Social Security disability payments, moved into a City Housing Authority three-room apartment in Harlem. It was, he said, "the hide-away I always dreamed of."

His first month's rent, $187.25, came from the Neediest Cases campaign, organized by *The New York Times.*

Without Albert Bishop's willingness to help himself, he never would have made it into that apartment. Without Ruth Francis's dogged determination, he would probably still be homeless. Without help from *The Times'* Neediest fund, all of the pieces of the puzzle might not have come together.

Every Person Who Perseveres Can Make a Difference

Every person can make a difference. The homeless, caseworkers, donors of funds – each person *who perseveres* plays a pivotal role in effecting change. Each person reading this book can make that difference.

Jewish sages teach us to look at the world as though it were perfectly balanced between good and evil. One good deed can tip the balance toward a better life. One evil act can destroy so much. A social worker, teacher, advocate for the poor, shelter volunteer or contributor to a worthy cause can be the right person in the right place at the right time—just as Ruth Francis was for Albert Bishop.

Amazingly, the opportunity to help can be as close as the street corner of any major American city. In March 1990, my daughter paused near Columbia University to purchase the latest copy of *Street News* from a homeless man. *Street News* is a biweekly publication intended to help the homeless help themselves. The vendor buys the paper for twenty-five cents per copy and sells it for a dollar. For every paper sold, the homeless also earn five cents deposited in a special savings account earmarked for rent. The vendor at Columbia told my daughter, "I have been able to rent a room on what I made selling *Street News*."

The idea for the paper came to Hutchinson Persons one day while walking through Grand Central Station. "What an untapped work force," he thought. "All these people just lying around here. But what can they do? This thought plagued me off and on, day and night, for about a week until suddenly it hit me . . . they could sell newspapers."[3]

According to Persons, founder and editor of *Street News*, a thousand homeless and nearly homeless men and women sold more than one million copies in New York City alone in the first few months of publication. Corporations such as Chubb Realty, Citibank and *The New York Times* have assisted.[4] A comparable publication, *Street Beat,* started up in Los Angeles in the summer of 1992.

The paper includes articles by celebrities and business executives and lists job opportunities targeted to the homeless. Help wanted ads seek distributors of flyers in Brooklyn, foot messengers on Wall Street and maintenance personnel for New York City's parks. Most of the employers require only a social security card and a letter from a shelter or soup kitchen, not difficult items for the homeless to obtain. I have written letters for several guests at my Temple's hospitality program.

It is no surprise that the operation bears no resemblance to a smoothly functioning corporation. But most of the *Street News* vendors I have met were energetic men or women who gained a new lease on life.

It is that energy that we need to bring to the surface. Each of us is a potential catalyst for the homeless. To be sure, not all the homeless are capable of working. But many are. How many Jim Robinsons, Gerald Winterlins and Albert Bishops are there on the streets and in the shelters of our cities?

They can be found in every state. In Minnesota, poor and homeless persons created a grassroots organization, The Alliance of the Streets, which began a job program that grew into a small business. They obtained a loan through the shelter where they were staying and then advertised services such as lawn care and cleaning. The business has expanded to painting, roofing and auto repairs. Workers earn at least $5 an hour. Equipment was purchased with the help of local churches.[5]

Human potential abides in the shelters of our land. When the homeless believe in themselves and when those of us who are able – and most of us are – lend them a hand, they certainly do not act like bums.

As I turn up the collar on my favorite winter coat
This wind is blowin' my mind.
I see the kids in the street with not enough to eat
Who am I to be blind?
Pretending not to see their needs.
A summer's disregard, a broken bottle top, 'cause they got
nowhere to go,
That's why I want you to know
I'm starting with the man in the mirror,
I'm asking him to change his ways.
And no message could have been any clearer!
If you wanna make the world a better place,
Take a look at yourself, and then make a change.

"Man in the Mirror," Michael Jackson

PART TWO

*The Homeless Remind
Us Of Ourselves*

4
THE HOMELESS REMIND
US OF OURSELVES

◆ ──────────────────────────────── ◆

"What makes my loneliness an anguish
is not that I have no one to share my burden.
But this: I have only my burden to share."
Dag Hammerskjold[1]

I have never been homeless. But I have often wondered what
it would be like to live night after night on the streets or in a
public shelter.

I spent a few nights sleeping at our Temple's shelter. They
were long and restless evenings, during which I awoke many
times flooded by sadness that decent men, women and children
were sleeping in our classrooms with all of their worldly
possessions crammed into shopping bags. When I returned to
my home early the next morning, I was overwhelmed with
gratitude for my abode.

I think a lot about how I would handle being homeless. I
realize that the world of the homeless is very far from mine –
but in some ways it is very near. No matter what our status, our
income or our neighborhood, we must all deal with tragedy and
bitter disappointment at some time in our lives.

When Tragedy Strikes, We Have Two Choices

We all have something in common with the Jim Robinsons, Gerald Winterlins and Albert Bishops of the world: each of us has a choice to make when we suffer a tragedy. We really have only two options: one is to be defeated by tragedy; the other is to be strengthened by it.

To be defeated means that we abandon hope in ourselves. In effect, we say that the loss of a spouse or a child, a severe physical disability or a job termination has finished us off, that we no longer have the power or spirit to do anything with our lives. Some homeless people go such a route of total despair. So do many of us. This attitude is guaranteed to cost us friends. Most people do not want to be around individuals who have given up. They can be so depressing that we wish to be rid of them as quickly as possible.

But there is another choice – the one Jim Robinson took: to be strengthened by tragedy.

How is it that tragedy inspires the human spirit? How is it that when we are deprived of what is dear, we so often find ourselves transformed into stronger, better persons?

I think it has something to do with being put on the spot. No place is left to which to run; we have to react. No longer can we put off the tough decisions that we have left to others or delayed and delayed and delayed.

One question overwhelms us at the moment of tragedy: that precious part of myself that I have lost – is it the totality of my life? Or am I left with enough to make it in this world? Can I find the strength to say that I may not have everything, but it's more than I really need to make it in this world?

I have a friend whose twelve-year-old daughter was killed while riding her bicycle. Shortly afterward, the woman contracted cancer, and, in order to save her life, her leg was

34

amputated above the knee. Yet with each tragedy, my friend became not weaker, but stronger.

How did she grow stronger?

Three Paths to Strength

First, as harsh as it may sound, she understood almost immediately that although she loved her daughter dearly and would have done anything in the world to save her, her daughter was *part* of her life, but not *all* of her life.

As for her leg, it was, to be sure, an integral and pivotal part of her body. But she learned that she could function well without the leg–driving, taking part in sports, traveling and so much more.

I remember visiting her in the hospital the day after surgery. We spoke about the operation and somehow I stumbled into asking her how she was handling yet another loss. I shall never forget her response. "Rabbi," she said, "that's not the question. The important question is, 'What am I going to do with what I have left?'"

Second, she quickly found ways of putting what she had learned to use to help others. Within months of her daughter's death, she and her husband were sitting in the living room of parents who had just lost a child, bringing comfort and insight to the newly-bereaved. And it was only one day after the amputation that she was counseling and inspiring her hospital roommate, helping her to deal with her own struggle against cancer.

After the initial shock, my friend never felt that she was useless or that her life was over. On the contrary, strength and wisdom she never knew she had surfaced from the depths of her being.

Third, she tried to put her life into some larger context, to see it as God might see it. That is not a simple task and most of us cannot do it by ourselves. My friend is no exception. She is bright, sensitive, well educated, but she needed help.

She got it from her religion, her faith and her community. She happens to be Jewish so she turned to the study of Torah (the first five books of the Bible) and its commentaries, to regular prayer and to the customs and traditions that have enriched Jewish lives for generations.

Had she been Christian, similar opportunities would have been available for her as they are for Hindus, Muslims, Buddhists and the adherents of other faiths.

A colleague of mine, a Protestant minister, told me about a member of his church who reminded me of Jim Robinson. Let's call her Betty. No, she was not homeless, but, like Jim, Betty suffered the loss of someone very dear – her nine-month-old son died of a genetic disease.

With the help of her pastor, a support group and church families, Betty gained an entirely new perspective on life. She began by looking back on her life before the tragedy and realizing how empty it had been. For most of her life she had done things because she was supposed to do them: she had a child, celebrated her husband's promotion, then had a second child so that the first would have a sibling.

When Betty's child was born, she knew almost immediately that something was wrong, but she did not know how serious it was. When it was time to baptize the child, she wrote some creative prayers that included references to the special nature of the infant and petitions for God's help. When the child died four months later, that special service in the church became a distinct source of comfort to Betty.

Now she sees life through the prism of her tragedy: she has learned that life is empty without some sort of struggle and feels a sense of compassion for people who have never had to deal with tragedy because they may not have the strength that emerges from struggling. Betty believes that she now lives her life on a deeper and richer level.

She has more in common with Jim Robinson than meets the eye. When Jim lost his friend on the beach at Atlantic City, he did not give up; he did not become a bum. He had a cause for which to strive and he became a stronger person. Yes, we have more in common with the homeless than we care to acknowledge.

In dealing with tragedy, we can choose to be defeated or strengthened.

That is the time to ask, "What can I do with what I have left?"

That is the time to tap our hidden resources.

That is the time to turn to other people, to the community and to religion.

When I hear the inspiring stories of what the homeless have done for themselves, I am reminded of what the rest of us are capable of doing. And when I see what members of my synagogue and my colleagues' churches have done to put the pieces of their broken lives back together, I realize the resiliency and the potential that we all have, including the hundreds of thousands who will spend tonight in a shelter, on the street, or in an abandoned car.

5
QUESTIONS WITH WHICH WE WRESTLE

◆————————————————————————◆

*"Whoever saves one life
saves the whole world."*[1]

*M*ark McGurl, a staff member of *The New York Times,* was approached one day by a homeless man: "Hey, man, could you lend me $5,000? My Porsche needs a new transmission."

Stopped in his tracks, McGurl turned and smiled. "Yeah, I hate it when that happens." Then he gave the man a few dollars. "It didn't help him with his Porsche and probably didn't get him any closer to having a roof over his head. . . . I didn't mind giving, it being late and the real world confusing."[2]

The real world of the homeless is confusing. Not only do professionals and volunteers involved with the homeless wrestle with difficult ethical questions every day – so does the average citizen who owns a home, rents an apartment, waits on a subway platform or just walks down the street minding his or her own business.

This chapter will examine some of the moral dilemmas that we all wrestle with when our lives intersect with the homeless.

Let's begin with a situation that almost every American adult has encountered. You are making your way down the street of your town and someone approaches you for money to buy a cup of coffee, a meal, a pack of cigarettes or a bus ticket to a town where "there are relatives who will help."

What are the thoughts that go through your mind at that moment? How do you decide how to respond?

I have conducted an informal study, asking friends and relatives what they think at that moment. Here are some of their replies:

"She needs it more than I."

"What will he do with the money? Drugs? Booze? Is there any chance he'll buy food?"

"I'll give to every other one."

"If I don't give, will he or his friends try to rob me?"

"Hey, fella, McDonald's is hiring."

"All I have is my train ticket home. I'm out of money."

"Does he really have a lame leg – or is he faking it to win my sympathy?"

"My emotions say, 'Give,' but my intellect says, 'Don't be a fool.'"

"My conscience says: 'Help the fellow out. I think I'm ethical. Here's my chance to prove it.'"

"I'm numb."

"My parents would be proud of me if I give this poor fellow something."

"My parents would think I'm crazy if I give. . . . "

"There is no way this person is ever going to climb out of the gutter. Why throw good money after bad people?"

"I've already given a dollar today and over five bucks this week. It's starting to affect my own budget."

"I help in other ways. I work at a shelter, support social agencies and pay taxes that go for welfare."

How do these responses compare to yours? Which ones do you feel good about and which give you a queasy feeling in the pit of your stomach?

We will deal with religion's response in the next chapter, but here are some ways that thoughtful people have handled some of these dilemmas. You may not agree with them, but perhaps they will help you as you wrestle with these ethical issues.

A Friendly Word,
Shelter Cards, Burger King

A leader of one of the national organizations for the homeless doesn't give money to someone whom she thinks looks intoxicated or seems to be on drugs. Of course, it is not always easy to tell the difference between intoxication and illness. Her purpose is to avoid doing more harm than good. Is it unethical to give money indiscriminately? Is it possible to make a quick judgment on the street as to whom to give and to whom not?

I know a woman on a limited budget who frequently responds, "I'm sorry. I wish I could help, but I don't have any extra money today. Good luck to you." What are the limits we should impose on ourselves? What would you think of someone who gave money to three people per block? What do you think of those who give nothing at all? Is a friendly word or a smile worth as much as a dollar?

The actor Danny Aiello never passes a person on the street without giving something. If he has no money he at least "gives them a word to let them know that I empathize. I never yell at them or say, 'Get a job.'"

Every day a blind homeless man recognizes Aiello by his aftershave. He says "Hi Danny" and "Thanks." Even though he hears no coins hitting his collection plate he knows that Aiello always gives a bill.

Amazingly, we can make quite a difference in the lives of the homeless when we use kind words, when we take the time to learn someone's name or when we demonstrate an interest in what they are doing. Remember, their ego strength is near zero and their self-confidence is nonexistent. Whatever we can say or do that gives them even an iota of self-worth will probably have some benefit.

Some people have developed creative, constructive responses. A member of my congregation who works in downtown Newark, New Jersey, carries cards listing the names addresses, and telephone numbers of three nearby shelters and feeding programs. He figures that if one in fifty of the homeless he sees heads for a shelter, he has done a good deed.

My daughter has a friend who always carries with him a supply of gift certificates from Burger King. When approached, he hands one out and points the recipient in the direction of the nearest fast food outlet. If he has no certificates, he may offer to take the individual to a nearby cafe where he pays the cashier in advance. In that way, he knows that his funds are used for food.

How Suspicious Shall We Be?

Suspicion is sometimes well placed. We do not want to be taken advantage of. Nor can we say yes to every request.

I used the "Burger King approach" one day when I received a call in my study from a man passing through town who claimed that he needed money for shoes. "My shoes have worn out and my feet are starting to swell. Can you give me $50 for shoes?"

I had grown weary of telephone scams. Clergy are considered

an "easy touch" and some of the best minds on the street have thought up schemes to convince us to guarantee checks, lend cars and wire money. Having fallen for a few of them myself, I become suspicious of every telephone solicitation and wary when a transient appears unexpectedly outside my study door.

"I can't give you $50 cash," I responded, "but I'll meet you and buy you shoes."

Certain that my caller would not show up at the shoe store, I nonetheless made my way downtown. To my amazement, he was there waiting for me – his severely deformed foot encased in a tattered shoe.

Since that day, I have often thought: what if I allow my suspicions and apprehensions to get the best of me? What if I stop seeing each homeless person as a child of God? What if all of us were to allow our confusion and our distrust to shape our responses to the needy?

Many of us do precisely that with our spouse, our children and our friends. Teachers do it with their students, employers with their employees and vice versa. We make quick judgments and we stereotype: my spouse is messy; this child is not athletic; that student never tries; my employer does not understand me.

We pigeonhole people. If we believe that our eight-year-old daughter has no talent for sports, we will probably not look for opportunities to develop her ability. We are then caught in a self-fulfilling prophecy. We predict that our daughter lacks the ability. We never give her a chance to demonstrate whether she has it or not. And then we congratulate ourselves on having made such an accurate prediction!

And so it is with the homeless. If we are convinced that they are all liars, ne'er-do-wells or alcoholics, we – citizens, agencies and the government – will treat them that way and that is what they will become.

Sometimes an encounter with the homeless can end in tragedy. It is extremely rare, but it does happen. And that single encounter can shape the attitude of an entire city.

Rodney Sumter, an unemployed construction worker, was standing on a subway platform with his three-year-old son at Columbus Circle in New York City when a homeless man spat at him and hit him for no apparent reason. Mr. Sumter says that out of fear for his life and that of his son he struck back at the man, killing him.

At the funeral for John Doe (no one knew his name), the national chair of the Congress on Racial Equality, Roy Innis, acknowledged that the millions who ride the subways and walk the streets do not know "how to deal with unpredictable and irascible homeless people like the man Mr. Sumter killed."[3]

New York City prosecuted Mr. Sumter for killing John Doe, but he was acquitted.

What conclusions should we draw from this unfortunate event? That we should avoid any contact with the homeless? Mr. Sumter was apparently minding his own business. That we should steer clear of confrontations? That is probably good advice in any public setting – on the street, in the subway or on the highway.

The conclusion that we should *not* draw is that homeless people are dangerous. On the contrary, they are probably among the least threatening group in our society. They are the victims of crimes, if anything, not the perpetrators.

Is Trespassing Justified?	◆	*It was a bitter cold night not long after Christmas and forty-four-year-old Benjamin Franklin Pierce decided to spend the night in his hidey-hole.*
		Most of the experienced homeless have one, a hidey-hole or a bolt hole, a sort of room in reserve for emergencies. You don't go there every
	◆	(Cont.)

44

night . . . you don't want to get rousted out of the place altogether by the owner or the police.

That's what happened to Mr. Pierce in December. He was arrested for trespassing. At first he planned to just plead guilty and take his chances, up to ninety days in jail.

But Vic Scutari, who runs a soup kitchen in Long Beach (NY), was outraged and suggested he fight.

"What was he supposed to do, freeze to death?" says Mr. Scutari, who feeds between forty and seventy people a day in Long Beach.

"On the night of Dec. 27," Mr. Pierce says, "it was very, very cold, and I had been all sorts of places, searching, and I was cut off.

"There was this building and I just went in and went to bed and the next morning the police officer came in and I was arrested. They said, 'Ben, you're going to freeze to death in here.' There was no hostility, no bad words."

Mr. Pierce had slept in the building before, an abandoned apartment house with a side door that is usually unlocked. The temperature was seven degrees, and the wind chill drove it to twenty-four below.

"There is no question he committed the misdemeanor of trespass," said Alan Levine, one of his lawyers, "but the law allows for a violator to be considered justified where the threat of harm to a person is greater than the harm involved in the violation."

Under New York law, such a violation is regarded as "justifiable and not criminal" when it is "necessary as an emergency measure to avoid an imminent public or private injury."

Said Douglas Colbert, Mr. Pierce's lead lawyer, since there are no homeless shelters in Long Beach, Mr. Pierce could either trespass in an abandoned building or risk freezing.[4]

Is Begging
Free Speech?

How much freedom are the poor and homeless entitled? In response to complaints, New York's Metropolitan Transit Authority sought in late 1989 to rid the subway stations of homeless beggars on the grounds that they interfered with the free flow of passengers and the safe and efficient functioning of the system. Begging was already prohibited on subway cars and within twenty-five feet of a token booth.

Federal Judge Leonard Sand ruled that begging in the subway is constitutionally protected speech. In effect, the Judge held that calling, "Any spare change?" is just as clearly free speech as "Give me liberty or give me death!" and that it is covered by First Amendment protection. He wrote that "it is the very unsettling appearance and message conveyed by the beggars that gives their conduct its expressive quality."

In a challenging decision, Judge Sand declared that "subways are public forums where the transit authority permits a wide range of solicitations by religious and social welfare groups. The authority would, in effect, have prohibited the blind beggar with a tin cup at his feet from soliciting along with the homeless panhandlers."

The Legal Action Center for the Homeless, which brought the suit, argued:

> Given the economic and political landscape of New York today, begging cannot be understood as anything but vital political speech. Every time a destitute person asks for change or extends a cup, he or she conveys the uncomfortable disturbing idea that in the midst of staggering wealth there live people who lack the means to live. If we silence the beggar by pushing him off the subways, we cut off one of his most effective channels of communication.[5]

The New York Times disagreed. It claimed, "Underground, at least, their right to beg is overridden by everyone's right to use the subway system in peace."[6]

In an insightful letter to the editor, Jean MacDonald of Brooklyn suggested that the real reason for banning beggars from the subway was not safety, but rather that "New Yorkers, the majority of whom have been brought up in religious and ethical traditions that make the care of the poor an obligation, want 'peace' from their guilty consciences."[7]

Is it true that we have guilty consciences about the millions of homeless who populate our cities and countryside? If we do not feel guilty about this situation, we should.

Is it true that we sense the gap that exists between our religious tradition and what is happening on our streets and in our subways? Like Ms. MacDonald, I am convinced that it is not safety or the unimpeded flow of subway passengers that we seek – but rather a respite from that gnawing conscience.

A Federal Appeals court overturned Judge Sand's decision, ruling that the ban on begging was constitutional. In a two-to-one decision, the court declared that "begging in the subway often amounts to nothing less than assault, creating in the passengers the apprehension of immediate danger." The United States Supreme Court agreed.[8]

Notwithstanding the decision of our nation's highest court, I still ask: who is assaulting whom? Is it not the homeless who are the ones being assaulted – by the lack of affordable housing and job-training programs?

> ◆ *Not for a minute should we concede that exist-
> ence in a cardboard box on a city sidewalk is
> "life" in the constitutional sense. Not for a mo-
> ment should we allow that a person without heat*
> ◆ (Cont.)

*or shelter during a freezing winter possesses "life,
liberty and property" in the constitutional sense.*
Charles A. Reich[9]

♦

What I Learned from Those
Aggressive Windshield Washers!

Perhaps it is good fortune that we must pass by the homeless on
our way to work – or even have our windshields involuntarily
washed. I must admit that those windshield washers used to
provoke wild rage within me. Why was I so angry with them?
Why did I feel my blood pressure rise as I waved them off? Of
course it was, in part, because they were imposing themselves
upon me, invading my private space and forcing me (and my
car) to submit to their wishes contrary to my will.

But now I perceive that other forces were at work within my
psyche. I usually drove into New York from the New Jersey
suburbs for cultural or social pleasures. Those men were there to
remind me that New York City is not only a cultural smorgas-
bord, but also a seething cauldron of poverty and homelessness
which no one, including suburban dwellers, can avoid. It was as
if the windshield-washers were standing there with a large sign,
reminding everyone who entered our big cities: "No one can
find peace until we all find peace."

They are like the canaries to which I referred in Chapter One.
As the canaries warned miners about dangerous gases deep in
the mines, so the windshield washers warn us that there is
something seriously wrong in our society.

My rage was also directed at a pervasive sense of helpless-
ness. Neither I, the religious community, nor our government
seem able to make a dent in the armor of poverty that encases
our cities. Most people seem to feel that the homeless have
become permanent fixtures in the landscape of our cities, like
high rises, newspaper stands, bulging garbage bags and frozen
yogurt shops.

Sometimes anger serves a social purpose. That was clearly true in the case of Mitch Snyder, who died on July 5, 1990, at the age of forty-six. His anger about the condition of the homeless in America fueled a national cause.

Throughout his life, Mr. Snyder was a troublemaker. As a teenager, he spent time in reform school for repeatedly vandalizing parking meters. As an adult, he was imprisoned for auto theft. But when he focused his anger on social injustices, challenging the conscience of indifferent officials, he was extraordinarily effective.

His antiwar sentiments led to a hunger strike that, in turn, helped persuade the Reagan Administration to change the name of a nuclear submarine from the Corpus Christi to the U.S.S. City of Corpus Christi. Snyder argued that no warship should be named the "body of Christ."

As director of Washington's Community for Creative Non-Violence, he engaged in a fifty-one day fast in 1984, finally persuading President Reagan to turn over an abandoned federal building for use as a homeless shelter. He often went without food or slept on sidewalks to dramatize the plight of the homeless.

His capacity for self-sacrifice and his visionary compassion set unusually high standards for all who care about decency and dignity for the dispossessed. [10]

NIMBYism – Not in My Backyard

But when I leave the city and drive back to the suburbs I find that fear of the homeless extends to every neighborhood of America – to the upper-middle class suburbs of Long Island and New Jersey and to the sprawling communities of Los Angeles. Wherever I traveled in the United States, I found men and women who wanted the homeless off the streets. Do something, anything, they insisted, but "do not put them in my backyard." NIMBYism – not in my backyard – is one of the pervasive themes in contemporary America.

In 1987, the Mayor of Los Angeles purchased 102 trailers to provide temporary housing for the homeless. Not wanting to concentrate them in a single neighborhood, he planned to distribute them among the various districts of Los Angeles, but, to his surprise, no one could abide them in his or her neighborhood.

NIMBYism engulfed the city as the citizens cried, "Not in my backyard."

Whether the homeowner resides in Albuquerque or Atlanta, we hear the same fears: "I've worked all my life to live in this pleasant neighborhood and I'm not about to let riffraff move next door to me and watch my property values plunge."

On a warm Sunday in March of 1990, I visited the Grammercy Place Shelter sponsored by Jewish Family Service of Los Angeles. I wanted to see for myself what happens when a well-run shelter is located in a middle-class residential community.

When I encountered difficulty locating the shelter, I stopped five teenagers to ask directions. "There's no shelter near here," one of the boys insisted. I persevered and soon discovered the shelter one block away! It had been there for several years, but not one of the youngsters knew about it.

No wonder! It looked like all the other residences – neat, clean, well-cared-for – except that it was actually one of the more attractive structures on the block. When it became a shelter, the building had received plenty of tender loving care inside and out.

Affluent Towns Avoid Responsibility

The same scenario gets played out in wealthier communities, such as Long Island's affluent Nassau County, which had not opened a single permanent housing site for its 15,000 home-less by late 1989. Concerned state officials encouraged non-profit agencies to apply for grants. An ideal site was located – a vacant six-unit apartment house in Roslyn which required no zoning variance and had a bus stop in front and a train station nearby.

Although no local approval was needed, the community agency nevertheless notified town officials and won the en-dorsement of the county executive and town supervisor, both Republicans, and the local Democratic assemblyman. The Junior League offered to furnish the kitchens, and, by December 1989, a state grant had paid for the building.

The residents also would be ideal: Roslyn families who were currently doubling and tripling up, such as Melody Miles, a twenty-seven-year-old data-entry clerk and single parent of two, who shared a single room in her grandmother's basement. A mentally ill cousin occupied the other basement room. Ms. Miles said that she walked by the building regularly. "I look inside trying to figure out how big the rooms might be."

But in January 1990, a new town supervisor, Ben Zwirn, was sworn in. Zwirn chose to oppose the building because a procedural error had been committed: the local civic association had not been informed before the purchase.

"My objections are not to the project. My objections are to the procedure. I'm very sensitive to that," explained Mr. Zwirn.

All that had remained for the homeless before they could move in was for the town board to agree to accept federally financed rent subsidies from the county. That's all – and a building vacant for three years would become home to men and women such as Melody Miles and their children, who were in great need.[11]

Zwirn and a council member eventually changed their minds and supported the plan, which was approved by a vote of three to two.[12]

Was the issue procedure or was it, once again, NIMBYism? The Roslyn proposal was particularly revealing because it was intended for the use of local residents who had been priced out of the local market. Is it our intention to force people to leave communities that they have lived in all their lives when property values skyrocket and affordable housing is no longer available?

> ◆ *To show that he cared about the homeless in general, Zwirn had a meeting of the clergy to encourage congregations to adopt homeless families. He suggested they get children involved "preparing books and toys for the homeless," adding, "We can feel good about ourselves if we get our children involved."*
>
> *Every clergy member said the same thing to him: "You want to create an adopt-the-homeless project, fine. But we still support the six apartments." Not one opposed the project. Zwirn's rabbi was among its strongest backers.*
>
> *The Rev. Stark Jones, whose Presbyterian church is in one of Roslyn's richest sections, has had homeless people sleeping in his steeple, the church study, the sanctuary floor. "When an opportunity like this arises we have to seize it,"*
> ◆ *he said.*[13]

In the landmark Mt. Laurel case, the New Jersey Supreme Court ruled that every community has a responsibility to provide a certain minimum of affordable housing. That was a profoundly ethical decision which set a new course for housing in the United States, a course that must be encouraged and maintained.

NIMBYism extends far beyond fear of the homeless. It has become a national preoccupation as communities struggle to "protect themselves" against people who are different. It has become a national paranoia and xenophobia.

What could be more compelling to the American people than cancer care? And yet, when Joan Kroc, the philanthropist and former owner of the San Diego Padres, wanted to donate a Ronald McDonald Camp Goodtimes for children with cancer, the citizens of Santa Barbara, California, were up in arms. Anything but the look-alike-three-bedroom house on a quarter of an acre still threatens the homeowners of America's cities and suburbs. We are creating a nation of gated communities – gilded and not-so-gilded – that lock out anyone who does not look like us, behave like us and feel as healthy as we do.[14]

The Underlying Fear:
Property Values Will Plummet

What underlies this broad opposition to the introduction of shelters, transitional residences, group housing, permanent low-income dwellings or a cancer-care facility for children in our local communities?

Most Americans fear that such arrangements will cause their property values to fall. To be sure, a family's home is usually its primary asset and concerns about its value deserve attention.

But are these fears justified? According to a 1988 State of California report, there is no statistical basis for them. In a survey of fifteen studies of low-income housing and property values,

> fourteen reached the conclusion that there are no significant negative effects from locating subsidized, special-purpose or manufactured housing near market-rate developments. Some, in fact, reported positive property value effects after locating subsidized units in the neighborhood.[15]

How much of this concern about property values has to do with race? The average American assumes that shelters and subsidized housing will be populated largely by blacks since blacks are over-represented among the poor. As noted in Chapter Two, the poverty rate for blacks, thirty-four percent, is three times that for whites.

Affordable housing and the enforcement of fair housing laws are interrelated. Some real estate agents find ways to avoid showing black families *all* the homes available in *any* neighborhood in their price range. And what about banks? Government studies through the 1980s revealed that blacks and other minorities had more problems than whites getting mortgages.[16]

On the other hand, there *are* neighborhoods that have deteriorated with the arrival of integration. How is it that in some communities deterioration has occurred while in others stability and economic growth have emerged? The answer usually hinges on whether or not the community was well organized to encourage integration. Where effective community-based groups existed, stable neighborhoods were maintained.

The same pattern is true in the development of low-income housing. As we shall learn in Chapter Ten, community-based groups that empower all the residents—low and not-so-low-income people alike— make a critical difference. There are many constructive steps that we can take to make it easier to integrate new kinds of housing into existing neighborhoods.

Most Americans whom I know are optimists. They believe that we will eventually reduce pollution, find a cure for AIDS and see democracy emerge in China. But strangely, they seem less sanguine about eliminating poverty and homelessness. I hear that we lack the will to do so, that our commitment to the homeless does not go much beyond shelters and soup kitchens, that too few citizens—in and out of government—are ready to take responsibility.

Is This the
Society We Want?

According to a study by the Congressional Budget Office, the poorest ten percent of American families saw their incomes drop by fifteen percent from 1977 to 1989. During the same period, the richest five percent had a twenty percent increase and the richest one percent had a seventy percent increase![17] The people who needed help the most in the eighties obtained the least. And those who needed it the least? You guessed it: they received the most.

Or look at it this way: the bottom forty percent of families earns less than twelve percent of all family income in the United States, while the top one percent receives 12.5 percent of all income. In other words, the top one percent has more income than the bottom forty percent and owns more wealth than the bottom ninety percent. The United States now has the worst inequality in income and wealth since the government began collecting such data.

The most distressing dilemma I wrestle with is that the rich are getting richer and the poor are getting poorer. We need to ask ourselves if this is the society that we want for ourselves and our children.

Judaism and Christianity have some important things to say about poverty, homelessness and our responsibility to those who are oppressed and downtrodden. We turn now to that message.

PART THREE
Working Together

6
WHEN ELIJAH KNOCKS

*R*eligion delivers a clear, unmistakable message about poverty, hunger and homelessness. It rings clearly in the Hebrew Bible, which is central for both Jews and Christians, and in the New Testament, sacred for Christianity.

Both religions teach that faith is not enough. Unless we translate our religious beliefs into deeds, they are hollow. The clarion call of Leviticus, "You shall love your neighbor as yourself," echoes through the New Testament.

In the Epistle of James from the New Testament, Christians are commanded:

> What does it profit, my brethren, if a man says he has faith but not works? Can his faith save him? If a brother or sister is ill-clad and in lack of daily food, and one of you says to them, "Go in peace, be warmed and filled," without giving them the things needed for the body, what does it profit? So faith by itself, if it has no works, is dead.[1]

An Inventory of Moments through Which We See God	◆	*Being in God's presence is not a matter of being in the right place, but of doing the right things. What must be happening in our lives for us to feel that we are in the presence of God? Prayer . . . is one answer. Love is another. Healing the sick or experiencing the miracle of our own bodies' healing can be answers.*

. . . . feeding the hungry, straightening the backs of the oppressed, securing justice for those who have been wronged – are all answers. Religion properly understood is not a series of beliefs about God. It is an inventory of moments in our lives, things we do and things that happen to us in which the person whose eyes are open will be able to see God.[2]

Rabbi Harold Kushner

◆

If we are going to wipe out homelessness, all religious groups must work closely with each other and with the public sector. No group can do it alone. If churches, synagogues and mosques are going to make an impact, interfaith efforts are indispensable. The purpose of this chapter is to help Americans of all faiths to understand how we are alike when it comes to helping the poor and the homeless.

Jews Know What It Means To Be Homeless

Jews know what it means to be homeless.

By the end of the Holocaust, six million Jews had been exterminated and millions more uprooted from their homes – from Germany, Austria, Poland, the Netherlands, Hungary, Czechoslovakia, Greece, Latvia, Lithuania, Romania and Yugoslavia.

Throughout their history, Jews have been forced to flee for their lives. Mass migrations of Polish Jews followed the brutal Chmielnicki massacres in Poland in 1648. By the end of that century, perhaps twenty percent of European Jews were home-less. During the fifteenth to eighteenth centuries, fifteen to twenty-five percent of the Jewish community were either pau-pers or unemployed.[3]

In 1492, the Spanish Inquisitor-General Torquemada pre-vailed upon King Ferdinand and Queen Isabella to issue a decree expelling all Jews from Spain. After more than eight centuries of residence there, hundreds of thousands of Jews were forced into exile. Some historians place the number of homeless Spanish Jews at 800,000.

Jews were no strangers to homelessness. In the centuries before the Inquisition, they had been expelled from England, Germany and France, even as they had known expulsion from their beloved Holy Land at the hands of the Assyrians, Baby-lonians and Romans.

The Jewish people was born at Mt. Sinai, during forty years of nomadic wandering. Having fled Egyptian slavery, they were a collection of uprooted people camped at the foot of the mountain.

Abraham was the progenitor of the Jewish people. He too had left his home, which was Ur of the Chaldees, and traveled west to establish a new tribal family in Canaan. The Torah describes him as *Arami oved*, a fugitive – or, as some translate, "a wandering Aramean."[4] The patriarchs, Abraham, Isaac and Jacob, and the matriarchs, Sarah, Rebekka, Rachel and Leah, wandered over much of the ancient world. When famine devastated Canaan, they were forced to leave home to search for food in Egypt.

When Elijah Knocks at Our Door

According to a Jewish tradition recited every year at the Pass-over Seder, Elijah the prophet was himself homeless, an advo-cate of the poor. Before he died, he announced that he would return once in every generation disguised as a poor oppressed person, arriving at the doors of Jewish homes. Elijah's treatment would determine whether humanity had improved enough to expect the coming of the Messianic Age. In this way the rabbis taught us that any poor or homeless person might be Elijah.

Christians have a comparable tradition. A saintly Irish Christian brother once said, "You've got to take care of the poor. You never know which one of them might be Him." A church member, volunteering one night at a shelter, described it as one of the profoundly spiritual moments of his life.[5]

People who serve in shelters report that they have found it to be not only a religious moment, but also a time when their own burdens are lightened and their personal strength and courage are bolstered. Perhaps this is what the Psalmist meant when he wrote, "Blessed is the person who considers the poor; the Lord will deliver him in time of trouble."[6] I have personally felt a strong sense of God's presence at shelters, in transitional housing and wherever men and women gather to help the poor.

Relationships with poor people are converting. My experience is that middle-class churches that open their hearts to the poor benefit at a deep spiritual level as much as the poor benefit from the bricks and mortar.

When our compassion for a specific individual or family causes us to ask why they have become homeless, we can begin to change the system that oppresses them while we work for their individual empowerment. Charity must always be coupled with justice if we want permanent solutions.

The congregations that developed housing
(Cont.)

62

ministries . . . have taken a leap of faith. We encourage you to join them in this journey. The rewards are great and life-changing.[7]

Rev. Keary Kincannon,
Director of the
Churches Conference
on Shelter and Housing

◆

Rev. John J. Steinbruck, who has done exceptional work with the homeless at the Luther Memorial Church in Washington, D.C., has taken the biblical image of the nomadic wanderers and placed them right at the doorsteps of our houses of worship.

> Our biblical Bedouin foremother and forefather, Sarah and Abraham, carried their tents as they nomadically moved from oasis to oasis. Not to be equipped with instant protection would mean death in the desert. And to encounter and welcome the stranger, offering refuge and thus survival, was the highest moral good. And it still is.
>
> Our cities today are choked with a new Bedouin type— the urban nomads. Often sick and always impoverished, they wander from place to place, seeking the resources for survival. Our urban asphalt deserts are no less forbidding than the biblical deserts.
>
> Jesus went even to the "far country" of the Gerasenes, to the shelter tombs in which the "demoniacs" and lepers were forced to live in exile, downwind from established society.
>
> Our church steeples need to be symbols of welcome to the stranger ("Come unto me. . ."). Each church or congregation ought to establish, at a minimum, one house for Elijah or Jesus, who may knock at any hour in need of refuge. Land for parking cars should be transubstantiated into lots for affordable housing.

This earthly refuge offers sufficient resources for all our needs, but not for the selfish greed that spawns homelessness. . . .[8]

The Midrash, a collection of stories and commentaries on the Bible, teaches the same lesson: "God stands with the poor man at the door and therefore we should consider whom we are confronting."[9]

Every opportunity we have to help the needy is a chance to encounter God *and* make a real difference in the world. The Talmud, the central repository of rabbinic wisdom, reinforced this idea:

Only a single person was created in the world to teach that, if anyone has caused a single soul to perish, Scripture considers it as though he had caused a whole world to perish. But if anyone saves a single soul, Scripture deems it as though he had saved a whole world.

The rabbis also taught that a single person was created so that no one should say to his fellow, "My father was greater than your father."[10]

God Stands with the Poor

Christians and Jews alike believe that every human being was created in the image of God.[11] For Jews, this does not refer to any physical likeness, since they try not to think of God literally in bodily terms. Rather, it refers to our moral conduct, which is supposed to resemble God's justice and compassion.

According to Deuteronomy,

"God upholds the cause of the fatherless and the widow and befriends the stranger, providing him with food and clothing. You too must befriend the stranger, for you were strangers in the land of Egypt."[12]

The New Testament does not mince words either:

> Bear one another's burdens, and so fulfill the law of
> Christ.[13]

Since God identifies with and cares for the downtrodden, we show our love for the Eternal by modeling our moral behavior after God. Isaiah taught that caring for the poor is an indispensable requirement for a life of piety. While Jews fast for twenty-four hours on Yom Kippur (the Jewish Day of Atonement), God reminds them that fasting is not enough:

> Behold, you fast only to quarrel and to fight
>   and to hit with wicked fist.
> Fasting like yours this day
>   will not make your voice to be heard on high. . . .
> Is not this the fast that I have chosen. . . .
>   to share your bread with the hungry,
>   and that you bring the homeless poor who are cast out
>   to your house?
> When you see the naked that you cover him,
>   and that you hide not yourself from your own flesh.[14]

In Christian tradition, John echoes the Hebrew prophet:

> If a rich person sees his brother in need, yet closes his
> heart against his brother, how can he claim that he loves
> God? My children, our love should not be just words and
> talk; it must be true love, which shows itself in action.[15]

The *Ethics of the Fathers* teaches that all our possessions belong to God: "Give unto God of what is God's, seeing that you and what you have are God's."[16] This is illustrated in a story told about Rava, a fourth century teacher. A poor man appeared before Rava, who asked what he usually ate. The poor man replied, "Fatted chicken and old wine."

"But don't you feel that you are a burden on the community?" asked Rava.

"Do I eat what is theirs?" asked the man. "I eat what is God's."

The message is clear: our resources belong to God. If we do not give to the poor, we are questioning God's authority and flirting with idolatry. The Talmud teaches that being hospitable to wayfarers is more important than how we receive the Divine Presence.[17] If we must choose between remembering God and taking care of God's people, our first obligation is to care for God's creatures. "A community that has no synagogues and no shelter for the poor must first provide shelter for the poor."[18]

God has given us the resources to support quite a large population on this planet. Not a limitless number, to be sure, but many billions. The challenge is ours – to allocate our resources wisely and avoid obscene disparities between rich and poor. There are communities where children die of hunger while a few miles away a family chooses between its Rolls Royce and Jaguar for an outing. Something is badly askew when such enormous social distortions prevail.

Blaming God

Some people blame God for poverty. They argue that if God is all powerful and merciful, then the Almighty should have created a world where there are no homeless.

Others argue that the presence of homeless people demonstrates that there is no Supreme Power, for if there were, God would certainly care enough to alleviate their plight.

In other words, either God is not compassionate, is not all powerful or does not exist. According to this reasoning, since the world is in such bad shape, God can be compassionate or omnipotent, but not both. Or God simply does not exist.

These arguments ignore two central ideas in liberal Jewish and Christian thought:

One, that God has created a world which is imperfect.

Two, that human beings are partners with the Divine in improving the world. In Hebrew, we use a compelling phrase to describe the purpose of that partnership: *tikun olam,* which means mending the world.

God purposely created a world and left a lot of important tasks for us. That is our purpose on earth – to help finish the job God started.

Dividing the Responsibility between God and Us

What is the division of the responsibility between God and us?

I love to tell the story of the Vermont farmer who earned enough money to buy a run-down, overgrown farm. He worked hard to return it to good operating condition. When it was flourishing again, the local minister happened by for a visit. He congratulated the farmer on the results of his labors and observed that it was wonderful to see what God and human beings could accomplish when working together.

Replied the farmer, "P'raps it is. But you should have seen this place when the Lord was taking care of it all by Himself."

This is where we find ourselves today. God has provided us with abundant resources. But the Divine seems to have left it up to us to find a just way to distribute food, medicine and housing.

We have done a lousy job of distribution. In 1975 the Catholic bishops of the United States wrote:

> Our faith teaches us that "the earth is the Lord's" (Psalm 24) and that wealth and private property are held in trust for others. We are trustees of God's creation, and as good stewards we are required to exercise that trust for the common good and benefit of our brothers and sisters. . . . While the Church has traditionally recognized the right to private property, that right is always subject to certain limitations.[19]

I agree with the bishops. We are using the right to private property to justify homelessness and poverty. That defense is unacceptable. Yes, the right to private property is essential to our social and economic life. But it is subject to limitations. The land is God's and we are God's trustees. We must use the land to serve God's purposes. It should be obvious that when we step over and around the homeless to walk through the cities of America, we have abused that right.

The prophet Isaiah warned us about this sort of abuse:

> Woe to them that join house to house,
> that lay field to field,
> until there is no room,
> that you alone may dwell
> in the heart of the land.[20]

A Question ◆	*How do you react to the statement: everybody*
for the	*should get one house before anybody gets*
Mind and Heart ◆	*two?*[21]

Presbyterians trace their roots back to John Calvin, who was "an urban refugee" in Geneva, Switzerland. As the Reformation took root and the convents emptied, he used his new authority to fill them with homeless people. Against that background, the Pittsburgh Presbytery affirmed:

> We, as Calvinists, approve of commerce, but we expect it to meet the criteria that it serve the public good. We take the real world seriously, assuming with Calvin that all human enterprise is tainted with evil—safe assumption—and Calvin set about to make the gospel relevant to the city of commerce in which he lived and labored.
>
> In Geneva, Christian concern for the poor, the sick, the orphan, the widow, the refugee was institutionalized in the diaconate and legislated by law. . . . Later Christians

68

lost the urgency of this need to plan so that suffering be met by rational methods of alleviation.[22]

Some religious groups have not lost that urgency. Consider the Roman Catholic religious order Sisters of Mercy. It was founded in 1831 by Catherine McAuley, who felt impelled to do something for poor women in Dublin, Ireland. In 1981, the Order took a courageous and far-reaching action: it sold the property it owned outside Washington, D.C. and dedicated most of the proceeds to the cause of "justice in housing."

With those funds, the McAuley Institute was founded in Silver Spring, Maryland. Its purpose: to provide technical assistance in housing development, advocacy training, a revolving loan fund and guidance to religious institutions that want to participate in the housing effort.

We need to regain a sense of urgency about the homeless and the nearly-homeless. Every day that we delay is one more day that we neglect our religious obligation.

That point was made with bold clarity in an advertisement, designed and sponsored by the New York City Mayor's Voluntary Action Center, that appeared in *Street News* and other newspapers. Under a sketch of Jesus of Nazareth (the most famous homeless man in history) we are asked, "How can you worship a homeless man on Sunday and ignore one on Monday?"[23]

How long are we going to put off bringing our religious beliefs into harmony with our actions? Every day that we delay is another day in which children are hustled from shelter to shelter and their parents slip further into the abyss of malnutrition, exposure and disease.

Tzedaka Means Justice

There is no word in Hebrew for "charity." The term that comes closest is *tzedaka*, which means, literally, righteousness or justice. Helping others is not a "choice" – it is an "obligation."

Jewish tradition has spelled out this obligation in clear, specific terms. When Jews were an agricultural people, the Torah instructed them to leave the corners of their fields for the poor at harvest time. If individual grapes fell during cutting, those, too, were for the poor.

Before Passover, a collection was made to provide flour for *matzah* (unleavened bread) for the poor. Any individual who resided in a town for twelve months was obligated to contribute or entitled to receive these communal funds, which were known as *me'ot chittim* – wheat money.[24]

In a more general way, Matthew makes a similar point: "If you salute only your brethren, what more are you doing than others?"[25]

Another ◆ **Question** **for the** **Mind and Heart** ◆	*Do you have more respect for a person who makes $100,000 a year or for a person who makes $10,000? What if the person who makes $10,000 works in a soup kitchen?*[26]

The Talmud taught that everyone was required to provide for the less fortunate – even someone dependent on charity had to provide for those suffering more than himself or herself.[27]

In the Gospel According to St. Mark, Christians learn about

> a poor widow who came and put in (to the treasury) two copper coins, which make a penny. And Jesus called his disciples to him and said to them, "Truly, I say to you, this poor widow has put in more than all those who are contributing to the treasury. For they all contributed out of their abundance; but she out of her poverty has put in everything she had, her whole living."[28]

During a visit to a Manhattan drop-in facility, I met a homeless man on his way to visit a homeless friend who had been hospitalized. He was carrying soda and a bagel, all the refreshments his strained resources would permit. Did he know or just intuit that according to Jewish and Christian tradition even he was obligated to give? You will find many examples in this book of generous acts by homeless people.

Whom To Help First and How Much?

We are often confronted with questions about how much to give locally as opposed to nationally or overseas. Jewish tradition states that our first priority is to take care of our poor relatives. After that, the impoverished of our own town have priority over those of other towns. (If someone is traveling in a strange town and runs out of funds, he is considered to be a poor man and we should help him, even if he has assets in his hometown.)

But ultimately we are all linked to one another. *Six Degrees of Separation,* a play that opened at Lincoln Center in New York in 1990, is based on the theory that each of us is connected to every other person in the world by not more than six relationships. For example, I may have a cousin in London who does business with a merchant in Japan who has an employee in Tanzania who has an uncle in Zimbabwe . . . and on and on until each of us is connected with every other human by not more than six steps.

Whether or not the theory is correct, it has become evident that we can no longer isolate ourselves from what is happening in South Africa or Kuwait, let alone on the other side of town. Can residents of Coral Gables, an affluent area south of Miami, ignore what happens in Overtown, a low-income section just north of the urban center? Can Upper East-siders in Manhattan feel immune from the events of Harlem and the South Bronx?

Some northern New Jersey towns tried "Greyhound therapy." They loaded their homeless onto Greyhound buses bound for Atlantic City! That's immoral and will not work. As New

York Telephone reminds us in its advertising jingle: "We're all connected!"

But our time and resources are limited. How do we determine our priorities and where to direct our energies?

Imagine that the telephone rings. The caller states that he or she represents the local Coalition for the Homeless and is soliciting your personal contribution. Assume that you are inclined to give. The first question that enters your mind is: How much?

Or another scenario: you are Christian and it is Christmas or you are Jewish and it is Yom Kippur. As part of your prayers and meditation, assume that you are taking a spiritual inventory of yourself. A similar question surfaces: Have I given enough of myself and my resources to those in need?

The Bible offers guidance, instructing us to give one-tenth of our income (also known as a tithe). According to the Talmud, ten percent is considered satisfactory; five percent is termed "mean" (today we would say "cheap"). In Usha in the northern Galilee around 140 C.E., the rabbis declared that twenty percent should be the maximum lest the giver become impoverished and dependent upon charity.[29]

The percentages may vary, but religious tradition clearly teaches that philanthropy is obligatory and that a significant portion of our income should be dedicated to the poor. Ironically, studies tell us that lower income people give a higher percentage of their earnings to charity than do those in upper brackets.

How many of us have ever given ten percent of income – or even five percent?

A fourteenth-century Spanish-Jewish writer, Israel ibn al-Nakawa, described a unique and dramatic custom observed by Jewish communal leaders in France. They instructed their families that

> their coffins be made out of the boards of the tables upon
> which they gave food to the poor in order to show that

no matter how high a man may reach, when he dies he
can take nothing with him except the good he has done
and the compassion he has shown to the poor.[30]

And what if a person can afford to give to the poor and does
not? According to the Talmud, the Jewish court may assess
someone who refused to give charity or who donated less than
his means allowed.[31]

Respect:
An Indispensable Ingredient

Even the act of giving was not sufficient. It had to be accompanied by the right attitude – respect. That is why the corners of
the fields were not presented *directly* to the poor, but rather were
left for them to gather without embarrassment to themselves or
their families.

In Talmudic times, it was a custom to announce that a meal
was in progress by displaying a flag.[32] In that way, the poor
transient did not have to ask for a meal; he had a standing (or
waving!) invitation. The medieval Jewish philosopher Maimonides taught that the best assistance was by means of a loan.

Acts of *tzedaka* were best if accompanied by kind words:

> He who gives a coin to a poor man is rewarded with six
> blessings; but he who encourages him with kind words is
> rewarded with eleven blessings.[33]

> ◆
> *If a poor person requests money from you and
> you have nothing to give, speak to that person
> consolingly.*
> *Maimonides*[34]
> ◆

Rabbi Abba used to wrap money in a satchel, which he
trailed over his shoulder. When he visited the poor, they could
help themselves secretly.[35]

This was their right: simply because they were human, they were entitled to those offerings and they were not at the mercy of or dependent upon the whim of the giver. Today we call these rights "entitlements."

In the United States today, decent housing is not an entitlement. This means that benefits are not made available to all who apply and are found eligible. It depends on whether Congress appropriates funds – a big "if," conditioned by the economic and political climate.

A Voluntary Tax on All Parties

I remember serving a meal one day at our Temple's shelter and then attending later that evening an elaborate party that must have had enough food left over to feed a small city of homeless people for a month. I was shaken by the juxtaposition of great wealth and abject poverty and how incompatible it was with Christian and Jewish tradition.

When we are judged in the world-to-come – or when we judge ourselves in this world by the religious values we espouse – how does our conduct stand up? Can we justify such a vast chasm between the poor and the well-to-do?

Centuries ago, Jewish charitable associations in Eastern Europe imposed fees for honors at synagogue services and assessments at banquets and family celebrations to support the poor. In our own time, MAZON, a Los Angeles-based national organization, encourages Jewish individuals and institutions to voluntarily give three percent of the cost of their bar mitzvahs, wedding celebrations or group-sponsored meals. With more than 800 synagogues embracing this program, MAZON disbursed $1.2 million in 1991 to the hungry and homeless.

How transforming for us and for those we help if we all voluntarily taxed ourselves three percent of our wedding, confirmation, bar or bat mitzvah or baptismal celebrations and disbursed those funds for the homeless. Anyone who spends $1,000 for a party can surely afford another $30 for the needy. And for the few among us who expend $10,00-$20,000, a gift of $300-$600 seems modest enough. Suggestions of agencies that will use your gift well can be obtained from your priest, minister or rabbi or in the Resource Directory at the end of this book.

Such a gift sends a powerful message to our children and grandchildren. How else do we explain to ourselves and our children – and, yes, to our God – that we can spend tens of thousands of dollars on lavish parties and luxurious autos and so little for the poor?

Some maintain that since government and mega-agencies are so involved our efforts no longer count for much, that homelessness is just too great a problem for individuals, synagogues and churches. Nothing could be further from the truth. Neither Jewish nor Christian tradition has ever relieved the individual or the local church or temple of their responsibility because "larger institutions" are supposedly doing the job.

The message of this chapter is that as Jews and Christians we are *obligated* to rescue the needy – and that by fulfilling that obligation we act as God wants us to. The message of this book is that only through creative partnerships that involve all of us will we prevail. We turn now to examples of interfaith partnerships that have literally saved the lives of thousands of men, women and children who live on the margins.

7
THE INTERFAITH PARTNERSHIP

◆ ——————————————————————— ◆

hurches and synagogues, working together, have done
more for the homeless than I would ever have imagined.
In New Jersey, one woman's vision harnessed an army of
caring suburban volunteers to provide cost-efficient homelessness prevention programs as well as shelter. In Los Angeles,
congregations with vision and courage have taken a few risks to
transform dilapidated hotels into clean, safe housing. These are
but two examples of hundreds of religious partnerships nation-
wide that are attacking the homeless problem acre by acre.

Let's start with Karen Olson in 1985. Her job with a New
Jersey pharmaceutical company brought her to New York City
once or twice a week. As she passed through the Port Authority
bus terminal, she noticed the growing number of homeless men
and women.

Unlike other travelers, Karen stopped to talk with them,
quickly learning that they were hungry much of the time.
Deciding that she ought to do something, Karen and her children made sandwiches in their Summit, New Jersey home.
Weekends, they traveled to the bus terminal to distribute them.

Among the homeless was a former English teacher whom

Karen's twelve-year-old son befriended. "How did this happen to you?" he inquired.

"I had enough money for food *or* shelter, but not for both," she responded. Since shelter was available in public areas, she chose to spend what little she had on food. When the boy made his weekend visits, she helped him with his English assignments. Contrary to our stereotypes, this homeless woman was a professional educator very much in touch with reality.

As Thanksgiving approached, Karen realized that the bus terminal was a terrible place to spend the holiday. So she invited half-a-dozen homeless to her home for a shower, fresh clothing and a delicious turkey dinner.

> *For I was hungry and you gave me food. I was thirsty and you gave me a drink. I was a stranger and you welcomed me.*
>
> Matthew 25

Mobilizing the Religious Community

Karen quickly grasped that weekly trips to the terminal were not enough. As an active member of her church and a committed Christian, she sensed that the religious community of Union County in Central New Jersey could be mobilized to assist the homeless.

The citizens of upper-middle-class suburbs such as Summit, Westfield and Cranford were sympathetic to Karen's cause, but had no idea where they fit into the picture. Most had not seen a homeless person on the streets of their colonial style picture-perfect towns. Nor did they have much contact with the "hidden homeless." Few suburbanites visited the railroad station or the soup kitchen of nearby Elizabeth, where local homeless people congregated.

But Karen had a vision. With the cooperation of local synagogues, churches, social service agencies and corporations, she launched the Interfaith Hospitality Network. It has become a model for communities in New Jersey, Pennsylvania, Ohio, Connecticut, Michigan, and Minnesota.

Before the Network's establishment, there were fifty shelter beds in Union County to serve 1,500 homeless. The Network added twenty-eight beds – a fifty-six percent increase in shelter capacity!

How did they do it? By recruiting twenty-four churches and synagogues to provide hospitality rooms, food and socialization for a full week, four times a year. The Network provides the guests, who are pre-screened, with linens and transportation and assistance with medical, employment, financial and housing needs. Its goal is to move every family into transitional or permanent housing as quickly as possible. It provides a subsidized halfway house for those who are ready to move on.

Host volunteers are drawn from seventy congregations. When Temple Emanu-El of Westfield hosts the homeless, over 100 volunteers are involved in a single week, cooking supper and breakfast, playing with the children, chaperoning overnight and taking care of any special needs their guests may have. The cost for the program is $7.20 per person per day compared to nearly $40.00 when the State of New Jersey provides comparable service in local motels.

In addition, the Network operates a homelessness prevention program which targets the most vulnerable part of the population – single mothers and their children.

◆ *Bonnie G. shared these thoughts about her experience with the Interfaith Network: Just because I'm homeless doesn't mean I am not a person like you. A lot of people think that being*
◆ (Cont.)

homeless means that you're a "low life" in society, but what people do not realize is that eighty percent of homeless people are homeless because of landlords' greed in raising rent. . . .

I left Elizabeth (NJ) a year ago because a man bought my home and knocked it down to build condominiums. To start a new life, I packed up my three children and moved to Keyport. I rented a whole house for $600. Everything seemed to be going great. But my landlord raised my rent to $1,200. I refused to pay and . . . he pulled the electrical box out, turned off the water and pulled the chandelier down. The landlord was locked up for vandalizing the house and the cops had me call Social Services and we were put in a motel. It had roaches, drug addicts, pimps and knife fighters. My own children found drugs there.

Then Laurie and Kathy from the Manor House Program . . . recommended the Interfaith Council. We have to move each month. However, we met some nice people who really want to help us. As a woman it's easy to lose your self-respect. Turning to drugs or alcohol isn't that unusual for someone who feels they have lost everything.

However, I'm going to make it because this program has helped me believe in God. I might not have the house I want, but He is giving me and my family a roof over our heads and hot meals.[1]

On May 16, 1989, Bonnie and her children moved into their own apartment in Rahway,
◆ *New Jersey.*

Trying To Live
What We Preach

Jews and Christians alike believe that we have to break out of the walls of our religious institutions and put our ideals to work in the real world of poverty, sickness and war. Without outreach programs to people in need, religion seems sterile. The hospitality program is an effective way of making religion a force for good in the world.

Each year, Jews sit at the Passover Seder dinner and read, "Let all who are hungry come and eat; let all who are oppressed find freedom this year."

Christians teach a similar message, modeled on the life of Jesus: "Foxes have holes, and birds of the air have nests; but the son of man has nowhere to lay his head." The first human problem that Jesus faced was a lack of shelter.

On the eve of Jesus' birth, Caesar Augustus ordered Roman subjects to return to their hometowns and pay a tax. As a result, in Bethlehem and throughout the empire, the demand for shelter increased, but the supply did not. Consequently, there was no room in the inn for Jesus and his family in Bethlehem. That is why Christians are taught to "see in the faces of homeless men, women and children the face of Christ."[2]

What an inspiring sight it is to see a family or individuals bear witness to their faith by entering a church or synagogue to work with the homeless or by lobbying their congressperson or by restoring an apartment.

We Americans speak with pride about our Judaeo-Christian heritage. Interfaith services, especially on Thanksgiving Day and Brotherhood Week, draw us together – for a few hours. But what about the rest of the year? I have learned more about my Christian brothers and sisters and their faith by working side-by-side with them on behalf of the homeless than by decades of Thanksgiving observances.

An Interfaith Miracle
on Skid Row

So have George Regas, Rector of All Saints Church in Los Angeles, and his neighbor, Leonard Beerman, Rabbi Emeritus of Leo Baeck Temple. In 1986 they brought their two congregations together to do something about an urban tragedy: Los Angeles' skid row. Sixty-five hotels in that fifty-square-block area were either being torn down, leaving thousands on the streets, or had deteriorated so badly that drug abuse, disease, prostitution and roaches had taken over.

Eleven thousand people live on Skid Row; 8,000 in SROs. Some are old or disabled. Others have entry-level jobs. Some are disoriented. All are poor. This is an anonymous, hidden community – people who stay in their rooms, out of sight, who have withdrawn from society because they are afraid. The majority are decent people who seek only a clean, secure and cheerful place to live for the $225 a month which they can pay for rent.

The two religious communities made an interfaith commitment to help these people on skid row. Out of that agreement, a separate corporation – Church and Temple Housing – was born. With funds from the James Irvine Foundation, a development consultant was hired and three buildings near Fifth and Main were purchased. With Las Familias de los Pueblos, a skid row social service agency, $7 million was raised from eight funding sources, including the California and National Equity Funds. The Funds sold tax credits to corporate investors in return for the guarantee that the housing they were developing would be permanently affordable to low-income people.

Why save skid row? Why not let commercial interests tear it down? Because this is housing of last resort for these residents. If they were dispersed from that compact area, they would spread out onto the streets of Los Angeles, where social workers would never find them, where finding affordable housing would be unthinkable. A renovated, secure skid row offers them hope that Los Angeles's streets could never provide.

Even so, what is a nice, prestigious church like All Saints doing on skid row? Here is the answer of Bill Doulos, Church and Temple Housing's on-site owner's representative:

> In addition to all the altruistic reasons . . . we are also try-ing to find meaning *for our own lives,* a secure sense of our own well-being in the hands of God; we are working out our own salvation; we are engaging in the most ancient tradition of our Judaeo-Christian heritage: like the Israel-ites wandering for forty years in the wilderness, we are searching for our own place of blessing in the Kingdom of God. That's what we are doing on skid row.[3]

What does being religious mean if not working with the homeless? What could better merit God's blessing than helping men and women get back on their feet? As a rabbi, I have learned that truth from the Bill Douloses of the world. If anyone is doing "God's work," they are.

◆

If you want to raise a man from mud and filth, do not think it is enough to keep standing on top and reaching a helping hand down to him. You must go all the way down yourself. Then take hold of him with strong hands and pull him and yourself into the light.

Rabbi Shlomo of Karlin,
private builder of
low- income housing

If you believe in the resurrection, you say "Yes" to your own lives and to the lives of the people struggling to survive on skid row. And if you want to see how brilliantly the light of the
◆   (Cont.)

resurrection shines, you take it to the darkest corner of the world.

> Bill Doulos, Director of the
> Church and Temple
> Housing Corporation

As a kid, I marveled at people who were visible and made a difference. As an adult, I learned a lot about what a Jew should do for the oppressed from my rabbi, Leonard Beerman.

> Steven Moses,
> past president,
> Leo Baeck Temple, Los Angeles

◆

By January 1990, more than 100 men and women (including fourteen couples) were living in skid row's renovated Genesis and Pershing Hotels. On the day of my visit, I met forty-two-year-old James, who was overjoyed to have left the St. George Hotel, where he had been paying $288 a month to dwell with roaches and rats.

Born in Chicago, he had come to Los Angeles fourteen years ago to work as a nurse's assistant. But a broken foot that required two screws left him partially disabled. James's only living relative is a handicapped brother in Pasadena. The new rent of $225 that James pays at Pershing is easier to handle on his relief check of $312 – plus $92 in food stamps.

Another resident, Brenda, offered to teach James how to sew – and how to cook in the hotel's spacious and bright new kitchen. He looked forward to those lessons and to group visits to the Los Angeles Music Center. He planned to take the test for a post office job: the same work his parents had done. As James proudly showed me his clean, sunny room, I sensed that these friendly, secure surroundings would go a long way toward getting him, literally, back on his feet.

I asked Bill Doulos to identify his most satisfying experience as director of this program. Without hesitation, he responded,

"The one-year sobriety party I just celebrated with Archie, who had sought help from Alcoholics Anonymous after moving into the Genesis."

Bill, who resided in the manager's quarters at the Genesis, showed us room 31, which belonged to Raymond. It was more than living quarters – it was a toymaker's workshop. Originally from Houston, the forty-seven-year-old man came to Los Angeles with twenty-five years experience as a draftsman and, before that, experience as a schoolteacher.

Expecting Los Angeles to resemble what he saw on television, Raymond was shocked by the drug-infested back alleys. But as long as he was there, he decided to stay downtown. "This is where I've staked my claim," he said. "I'd like to make a difference here."

Carving Rocking Horses
at the Genesis

Raymond has made a livelihood for himself at the Genesis by carving rocking horses – an ebony steed with an ivory yarn mane, a white stallion and a cream-colored pony. His horses were auctioned for $175 and $225 in February 1990 at a benefit dinner for the Chrysalis Center, the downtown agency that helped him find his room. He'll use his share to purchase power tools to accelerate the drilling and sanding of the horses, which he had done by hand.

My image of men and women "hanging out" in shelters waiting for their lives to run out was shattered as I sensed the energy emanating from room 31.

Two residents at the Genesis have asked Raymond to teach them his craft. He hopes "to leave a little business" one day to his son, who is working his way through college.

"I believe the Lord is leading me now," says Raymond. "I wish I had done what I'm doing now twenty years ago. It wasn't my time back then, but now things are different."

The Glow on
Main Street

One night Bill Doulos was awakened by some noise at 4 a.m.
As he looked out the window, he saw only a solitary individual
at the end of the alley lighting up crack. He knew it was crack
because that substance has a characteristic glow that lasts thirty
seconds.

For years crack has been the only glow on skid row. Now
church and synagogue partnerships have ignited a new flame of
hope – not only for the tragic figures on Main and Fifth, but for
all of us.

> ◆ *The Skid Row Housing Trust might have been*
> *able to buy all the hotels without the assistance*
> *of religious groups. But churches and syna-*
> *gogues bring enormous resources we could never*
> *tap ourselves: therapists, pot luck suppers,*
> *fishing trips and . . . stability.*
>
> *Some of the Trust's mortgages will run for*
> *fifty years-we hope in perpetuity. To whom*
> *should we entrust such a precious resource?*
> ◆ *Obviously, the churches and temples are the*
> *best guardians.*
>
> *Inspired by this model, other churches and*
> *synagogues are entering in the "renovation pipe-*
> *line" at the rate of about ten a year. By 1995, all*
> *65 hotels should be purchased, renovated and*
> *managed with the help of the Skid Row*
> *Housing Trust.*
>
> *Sister Alice Callaghan,*
> *Director of*
> *Las Familias de*
> *Los Pueblos,*
> *a skid row social service*
> *agency in Los Angeles*

The Special Role of Black Churches

Black churches, one of the few stable institutions in the urban areas, are leading the way in rehabilitation.

They form the core of the Brooklyn Ecumenical Cooperatives' housing program. In 1983, after five winters of operating a shelter, forty churches and a synagogue agreed to move beyond crisis intervention to create permanent low- and moderate-income housing in Brooklyn neighborhoods. And what a need they filled! *Ten thousand families* applied for *113 units* of low- and moderate-income dwellings.

The ecumenical group established a credit union that extended construction loans and mortgages. In 1990, it launched a bank that will support a $200 million plan to redevelop an entire community, including the addition of several thousand housing units and job-generating industries. Roman Catholic institutions have provided $2 million in seed money.

Some churches operate programs under siege-like conditions. "Our House" is the name of a twenty-tow-bed shelter run by the Pomona (California) Council of Churches. It is full every day. No wonder! A city with 3,000 homeless, half of Pomona's citizens live below the poverty level. Most of those are spending seventy to eighty percent of their income on housing.

"These people have few options," said Pat Irish, the Council's Executive Director. "There's little talk about building affordable housing. Property costs are just too high here."

As I spoke with Irish, a shelter coordinator was in the next room negotiating with a landlord, appealing to him not to raise rents. "Since profit is his motive, are you ever successful?" I asked. "Oh, yes," Irish replied. "We appeal to their humanity and sometimes we succeed."

It was Junior Prom night, so one of the 125 volunteers was helping a young woman with her hair. "We care about the total person here," Pat Irish emphasized. "We run a job preparation workshop. We won't let them take a job at minimum wage, because at that wage they'll end up back at the shelter and we've accomplished nothing. They must make at least $6.00 an hour."

A refuge for poor people after the 1968 Watts riots, Pomona now sometimes resembles a battlefield. "Last week my shelter coordinator took a woman to see a house for rent," related Irish. "On return, she reported how pleased she was that it was on a cul-de-sac, which meant that it would be harder to have a drive-by shooting."

How do you concentrate on affordable housing when your biggest fear is drive-by shootings? According to Pat Irish, a child is shot almost daily in Pomona.

She had just returned from an interfaith mission to El Salvador. I was shocked to hear her say, "I saw religious hope there that I don't see here. The everyday person feels God is with her. I don't see that here. They have learned not to trust. But this is a place to trust."

The Religious Community:
a Safe, Trusting Place

The religious community offers a safe place where frightened people who have nowhere to turn catch a glimmer of hope and start to rebuild some sense of their own worth. The worst aspect of being homeless may be losing faith in oneself.

In October 1988, Willie D. Gatson and his wife, Shirley, were broke, unemployed and had nowhere to live. After losing the job he had for ten years in a Shreveport, Louisiana, bank and trying for eight months to land a new job, he and Shirley, her mother and their four children left that economically struggling region and headed for Atlanta with their $400 life savings.

After living with a friend for a week and then on the streets, they found their way to the winter shelter established by The

Temple. The shelter was founded in February 1984, after forty people had died on Atlanta streets from exposure.

"I feel the Temple is one of the best things happening here in Atlanta," said Mr. Gatson, "because of what it offers couples. It's clean, it's convenient and comfortable; the food is good and the people are friendly.

"For those people who had low self-esteem, they were there to uplift it. It gave you a boost . . . which allows you to say, 'Hey, I can make it. People do care.'"

After nine months in transitional housing, the Gatsons rented a three-room townhouse in southeast Atlanta. Mr. Gatson found work as a machinist at Brinks, Inc., and as a part-time radio announcer. Ms. Gatson is a housekeeper at Grady Memorial Hospital.

Operating on a $40,000 annual budget, the Temple shelter offers couples free medical and dental services, legal and vocational counseling, job referrals, professional grooming advice and counseling for marital and other personal problems. The shelter stocks condoms to assist with family planning.

Eighteen percent of the shelter's clients find transitional housing and employment, which may not seem like a great success. But measured against what happens without this support, it is quite an achievement. To assist couples who can make the transition to their own residence, The Temple subsidizes security deposits and moving costs. [4]

An Early Flight;
a Search for Meaning

I recall chairing a meeting in New York City attended by an Atlanta attorney who informed me that he intended to leave our session early to catch a mid-day flight back to Atlanta to serve meals at the shelter. "Chuck," he said in his Southern drawl, "I wouldn't miss that commitment for anything. Nothing I do is more important."

What is so significant about serving shelter meals that this attorney would shorten his trip? Could it be that with all of his success – financial, professional, personal – there remains an emptiness that does not let him rest? After all the vacations we take, the material goods we acquire, the honors we accumulate, do we sense that there is something else that we need to do to make our lives complete? Could it be, like Bill Doulos, that all of us are searching for meaning in our lives, for that "secure sense of our own well-being in the hands of God"?

8
LIFELINES

◆———————————————————◆

No matter what you do for a living or as a hobby, you can help the homeless. You might be a camera buff, mail clerk, attorney, physician, teacher or a shoeshiner. No matter what— there is a way that you can make a difference.

Your friends or associates may try to discourage you. How many times have you heard someone say about the homeless, "There's no helping *them*"?

But many can be helped—if someone cares enough to throw them a lifeline.

Binding Together (BTI) does exactly that. Since 1988, it has trained several hundred homeless men and women—*each of whom has a history of substance abuse*—to operate industrial capacity copy and binding machines. BTI, which grossed over $250,000 in its first year, provides hands-on instruction in its fully equipped facility. The trainees are referred from residential drug treatment centers and must be drug-free.

Funded in part by state and city agencies, BTI enlisted the support of corporations, which donated equipment, provided representatives for BTI's board and agreed to utilize BTI's copying services—and, most important, to hire its graduates.[1]

What a Days Inn Exec
Learned at a Shelter

After helping out at shelters and soup kitchens, many volunteers ask themselves: where do we go from here? If we maintain shelters indefinitely, aren't we insuring that homelessness will continue?

There is a syndrome called "shelterization." When homeless people live month after month by the rules of the shelter, they often lose their will to return to life outside. According to Dr. Paula Eagle, a Columbia University psychiatrist, "The shelter becomes your permanent home, instead of a stop on the way back to having your own room and job."[2]

Bill Hodges, a Days Inn motel chain executive, became acquainted with homeless people at the Atlanta shelter where he volunteered. Sensing that the homeless could be trained as reservation clerks, he convinced Days Inn's CEO, Michael Leven, to visit the Atlanta shelter.

"When you get into a shelter and look at the homeless," said Leven, "they appear absolutely normal. These people aren't dirty or falling off their feet drunk. They're everyday people who are down on their luck."

But Leven was so impressed by their desire to change and hold full-time jobs that he established a special program where the homeless receive social security cards and one-on-one computer training. Housing is provided at a local motel at $10 a day, with the company paying half. The clerks earn $5.50 an hour, receive health benefits and have promotion opportunities. Since the program began, dozens of people have maintained their positions, some have dropped out and the turnover rate is less than that of other workers for Days Inn.

If we don't rehabilitate these people now, argues Leven, we'll lose them forever. We will create a homeless class the same way we made a welfare class – a group of underprivileged people outside of society.[3]

If shelters are band-aids for the homeless, programs like Days Inn's are lifelines.

Lifelines are also furnished by a growing cadre of health care providers who save lives every day by specializing in service to the homeless. One of those is Dr. Mark Dollar, who reported:

> I see a lot of infected cuts on feet. If a person lives in a house, you give him a prescription for antibiotics and tell him to stay off his feet and change the dressing twice a day. That's really impossible for the homeless. So they end up in the hospital really sick a week later when the infection has spread.[4]

Another health care provider active in issues involving the homeless is Dr. David Woods, director of the Los Angeles Health Care for the Homeless Project: "You have to put disease in the context of homelessness. You don't send a homeless diabetic out of the hospital on insulin. He can't refrigerate it. He'll get mugged for the needles, and on insulin if he can't get food, his blood sugar will drop too low."

These physicians see a high incidence of the AIDS virus, foot problems and serious respiratory illnesses such as tuberculosis and pneumonia. Their efforts to treat these ailments among the homeless have their roots in demonstration projects funded by the Robert Wood Johnson Foundation and the Pew Charitable Trusts.

Lifted up by
Their Bootstraps

I still hear the chorus of voices of those who have made it in America – especially the voices of immigrants and their children ringing forth: "We pulled ourselves up by our bootstraps. Why can't *they*?"

Hank B. decided that instead of offering a handout every time he passed a homeless person downtown in a major East Coast city, he would employ them for his outdoor shoeshine business. They would pull themselves up by other people's bootstraps.

His recruits were given a shower, a tuxedo and a portable stand. In the summer of 1985, a municipal social worker started referring homeless people to him. Citing an 80-year old ordinance prohibiting "bootblack stands on public space," the local police shut him down. He tried to run the business in a hotel basement, but the rent was too much for him.

An agency working for civil rights filed suit on behalf of Brown and two homeless employees. A year later, a federal court declared the shoeshine ban unconstitutional and Hank and his crew were back in business.

Homeless people can do wonders with their hands and minds – but without a lifeline from business, medicine or law, they cannot overcome the terror of the streets or the obstacles of the city.

Collecting bottles and cans is the only "job" to which some homeless aspire. But it is an honest job that requires initiative. They were helped by a 1983 Returnable Container Act of New York State which required stores to accept up to 240 reusable cans and bottles per day from any single collector. The collector receives five cents per container. It not only serves the environment, but it provides homeless people (who can gather as many as 500 per day) with a little income.

But most of Manhattan's supermarkets – including A&P, D'Agostino's and Food Emporium – would not accept 240 cans. What does a homeless person do when stores flaunt the law?

Enter Doug Lasdon, executive director of the Legal Action

Center for the Homeless. Using New York University Law School volunteers and homeless collectors, his investigation revealed that ten stores would not take a single can and that the most any would take was sixty. The stores even posted signs announcing their limits–in direct defiance of the ordinance. According to Lasdon, "The stores have been able to get away with this because the people they hurt are the homeless, who are a low priority."

Lasdon brought a class action suit on behalf of the homeless and obtained an injunction. The stores quickly agreed to abide by the law. Without a lifeline from the Legal Action Center, another path of hope for the homeless would have been blocked.[5]

Reaching the Homeless with Books and Cameras

Mary T. is a children's book editor at a major publisher. Troubled by the large number of homeless–especially children–whom she encountered on her city's streets , she decided to do something to help them. Drawing on her own talents and experience working with autistic children, she created a small library at the local family shelter.

With the help of four coworkers she reads stories aloud, has the children read to each other and arranges for them to borrow the books. She believes that reading can give young people a sense of confidence and a head start.

Every one of us has something we can give the homeless–even if it is only a warm smile. Whatever our talent may be–cooking, repairing, gardening, photography–we can use it for the homeless.

Take Jim Hubbard, a Washington, D.C., professional photographer whose specialty is photographing the homeless. Tap ping his own skills, Hubbard created "Shooting Back," a program that teaches homeless children photography.

He takes eight homeless children each week through Washington's streets, teaching them how to use a camera. The kids rarely photograph images of decay, usually shooting playful scenes. A typical photo shows joyful faces jumping into the spray from a fire hydrant.

Why does Hubbard teach children photography when what they need is shelter? Hubbard says that housing is not enough; self-esteem is paramount. When children master the camera and see their photos in print their confidence levels soar.

Good Workers
in Unlikely Places

Here's an unlikely classified ad placed by a service corporation:

HELP WANTED
General Office Work. Welfare recipient, parolee, ex-addict OK. Good salary, benefits. Will train.

That's the way one company's supported work program invites the "unemployable" to learn to work for a living. Participants in the program include former offenders, high-school dropouts and youths caught up in the criminal justice system.

Best of all – it works! More than half the people who sign on do find permanent, well-paying jobs often in maintenance, construction, clerical or security work.

Barry B. had acquired some medical and office training during eight years in the U.S. Army. But personal problems and difficulties with the law kept him unemployed for some time. Once the company threw him a lifeline, his life turned around. He is earning college credit while he works full-time as a medical assistant. The service corporation has placed homeless people with banks, the IRS, municipal departments, and universities.

Everyone of us is a potential enabler. I have seen volunteers such as Mary T. sharpen the imagination and the reading skills of homeless children with two tools—books and a desire to help. I have seen business executives such as Michael Leven give homeless adults a chance to be trained for a new life.

Rabbi Tarfon, Jewish sage, once taught, "You are not required to complete the task. But neither are you free to desist from it altogether."[6]

Everyone has at least one lifeline to throw the homeless. How can we not offer it?

PART FOUR

Doing The Job

9
HOW TO PREVENT HOMELESSNESS

◆————————————————————————————————◆

atherine Martinez shed tears of joy as she thanked the
men and women who had come to help build a home for
herself, her husband and their six children, ages five through
eighteen. The scene was lunch break at the Chimayo Holy
Name Roman Catholic Church in New Mexico as the volunteers introduced themselves to each other – members of Episcopal, Methodist and Presbyterian churches in the nearby towns
of Los Alamos, Santa Fe, White Rock, Española and Santa
Cruz.

The Santa Fe chapter of Habitat for Humanity was in the
midst of its fourth project in two years. Habitat got its start by
renovating one home and moved on to constructing a small
house, followed by a slightly larger three-bedroom ranch. Now,
on a sun-drenched Saturday, a two-story, four bedroom home
with a spectacular view of the Sangre de Cristo Mountains was
going up on a hillside twenty miles north of Santa Fe.

What set this scene apart from most of the others we have
looked at is that the Martinez family was not homeless – at least
not quite yet. Their family of eight, including four children and
Catherine's parents, lived in an 800-square-foot trailer at the

foot of the site. Their living conditions had become intolerable, putting the Martinez family at great risk of becoming homeless.

Our focus in this chapter is homelessness prevention. Habitat for Humanity does prevention work most effectively and is an example of the finest use of community resources. Caroline Miller, chair of Santa Fe Habitat, had expected thirty workers that day. Sixty showed up, including the Vietnam Veterans of New Mexico. Most came out of religious conviction: "It just seems the right thing to do. It's what my faith teaches me to do," said a woman in her sixties from the White Rock United Methodist Church.

Santa Fe Habitat, acting as the bank, will hold a no-interest loan on the house. As the Martinez family makes its monthly payments, the funds will be recycled for Habitat's next construction program.

Catherine's husband, Robert, a Vietnam veteran suffering from post-traumatic syndrome, receives $19,000 a year in disability benefits, placing them below the poverty level for a family of their size. Catherine and their two oldest children were on the building site cutting wood, painting and landscaping the upper terrace.

There's Nothing Better Than to Give to Others

"I'm overcome with emotion," said Catherine. "The going was rough, but my faith in God carried me through. There's nothing better than to give of yourself to others." Then she gestured to a woman who lived in the home which Santa Fe Habitat had just completed. "Joan's here today, building my house – and I'll be at the next one that Habitat builds."

> ◆
> *It is one of the most beautiful compensations of life that no man can sincerely try to help another without helping himself.*
>
> *Ralph Waldo Emerson*
> ◆

It was time for Catherine's seventeen-year-old daughter to introduce herself to the group. "You're building our house, and we appreciate it more than you can ever imagine," she said as her voice cracked with emotion and her face broke out in a broad smile.

Since leaving office, former President Jimmy Carter and his wife, Rosalynn, have spent one week every summer working on a Habitat project, one of over 10,000 dwellings built or rehabilitated worldwide through 1991. The average cost to a family for a Habitat home in the United States is $30,000, plus 500 hours of "sweat equity," their own physical labor and their commitment to help construct future projects. Typical payback on the no-interest loan is $150 a month, manageable even on a very low income. Overseas houses range from $1,000 to $3,000. By 1992, Habitat had 707 affiliates in the United States and projects in twenty-six developing countries.

"Simple and decent" is the motto describing Habitat's housing goal. Applicants are carefully screened and have a strong vested interest to succeed. Of the six houses originally built in Atlanta, each one was still occupied by the original owner as of 1990. (The one-hundredth Habitat home in Atlanta was completed in early 1991). If a family wants to move out, they must sell the home back to Habitat at the purchase price, so that another needy family can be helped.

Habitat accepts no government money, although land grants, street pavement and sewer hookups are appreciated. Funding comes from individuals, churches, corporations and foundations.

Habitat is an ecumenical Christian housing ministry inspired by Koinonia Farm, an integrated, self-sufficient Christian community in poor, rural south Georgia. By having needy and affluent people work together in equal partnership, Habitat not only erects houses, but also builds new relationships and a sense of community. Because homeless people help to build their own residence, they have a strong sense of responsibility and empowerment to improve other aspects of their lives.

"We're not caseworkers, we're co-workers," declared Millard Fuller, Habitat's founder. And that's exactly the way it was on that picturesque New Mexico hillside when sixty volunteers joined Catherine Martinez and her family in building a new life.

People Who Make a Difference

♦ *Millard Fuller was a self-made millionaire at age thirty. After a stint at the University of Alabama Law School, he made a fortune selling cookbooks by mail and promoting fund-raisers for schools. With a luxurious home, a lakeside cabin, two powerboats, horses and a Lincoln Continental, he was also a workaholic whose health was deteriorating.*

One day his wife Linda announced that she was leaving him because of her rival—which was not another woman, but rather, Millard's obsession with money. After entering marital therapy, Millard made a dramatic proposal: sell the business, donate huge sums to charity and retain a few thousand dollars to start life over. This time they would base their lives on Christian principles. Linda agreed.

In 1976, Millard Fuller founded Habitat. In 1989, he received a salary of $14,300. His commitment to living with less was fueled by St. Augustine, who said, "He who possesses a surplus possesses the goods of others." To which Fuller added, "That's a polite way of saying that anybody who has too much is a thief."

Millard Fuller preaches the "theology of the hammer." He insists that "believing in Jesus has got to be more than a verbal proclamation. If somebody says in a sermon, 'Love your neighbor as you love yourself,' everybody would say,

♦ (Cont.)

104

> *'Amen!' When you look at the reality of their lives, though, they are laying up big, big treasures for themselves, but are not willing to be*
◆ *that concerned for their neighbors.'*[1]

Transitional Housing
Puts Families Back on Track

Habitat set a new world record in blitz building when 250 professional builders from the Nashville-Middle Tennessee Association of Homebuilders erected a home in five hours, 59 minutes and 59 seconds. In an expertly choreographed event on October 11, 1990, they completed the house in every detail, including painting, landscaping, a front porch swing and a flag.[2]

But there are not enough Habitat projects to serve every family at risk. A variety of approaches is required, depending upon the problems and resourcefulness of the family and the community. One of those is transitional housing.

Until Jeanette Veldhouse-Sellier's twenty-two-year marriage ended in divorce, she never imagined that her middle-class family would ever be on the verge of homelessness. How did it happen? Her husband walked out of their Minneapolis suburban home, leaving her with two children, thirteen and eighteen. He promptly lost his job, which meant that alimony and child support ceased.

Jeanette, who has a degree in child psychology, lost her well-paying position as director of a learning center. The best work she could find was at $5 an hour.

Once she exhausted her meager savings, she fell behind in her mortgage payments. Although her mother helped out, she felt too embarrassed to seek help from other family members.

She was within ten days of eviction when she sought help from the Elim Transitional Housing program, founded by Sue Watlov Phillips in 1983. Starting as a shelter at the Elim Baptist

Church, it evolved, with the help of the local utility, North States Power, into a transitional housing program which had benefited 5,000 people by 1991.

What did Elim do for Jeanette? It put her in touch with the county assistance office, which provided her with a security deposit for an apartment. Elim covered part of the first six months' rent. A small rent subsidy is a cost-effective way of keeping people on their feet and off the street. Elim directed her to food banks for groceries, a medical clinic and a fuel assistance agency that helped with oil bills.

Jeanette—who was within days of being homeless—is today the administrator of a youth program. "You think of the stereotypical homeless person as someone of low income who doesn't have an education and who's probably anti-social," Jeanette says. "But we're a middle-class American family. Without Elim's help, we'd have had to live on the streets."[3]

Elim's success is being duplicated across the nation by hundreds of community-based groups. Any city or suburban cluster of 50,000 or more people either has such a group or has the potential to create it.

| *A Woman Who Made a Difference* | ◆ | *Sue Watlov Phillips is a woman who made a difference. Born with a physical defect that left the right side of her body partially deformed, she knew what it was to be disappointed.* |

An avid athlete who earned a letter in every high school sport, her dreams of competing in the Olympics were shattered when she permanently damaged her knee playing basketball. "Everything I had worked for in my life was suddenly taken away," Sue recalls.

She dealt with that loss by working in children's shelters.

When a local shelter for the homeless closed, she embarked on "an educational and lobbying blitz" to convince her church, Elim Baptist, to convert empty space into a shelter.

But she quickly learned from the homeless themselves that what they needed most was transitional and permanent housing. By 1991 Sue had turned her physical disappointment into a future of hope for the 5,000 people who benefited from the Elim Transitional Housing Program.

Sue has a private therapy practice now, but she still works with Elim thirty to forty hours a week. One of the homeless Sue helped was Dan, a skilled builder who slept in warehouses. Today, he and Sue share a home; they were married a few years ago. Where? At the Elim Baptist Church, of course.[4]

Without a Voice Many Will Be on the Street

◆

Betty is a German Jewish woman, a Holocaust survivor in her late seventies, who is one crisis away from being homeless. Her late husband was an accountant and they always enjoyed a steady income. Today, she lives by herself in an SRO at the Hotel Euclid on New York's Upper West Side.

The owner, who wants her out, harasses her by "forgetting" to deliver her mail, telling visitors that she is not in or yelling at them to go away. There is no lock on the door of her room and with broken windows, pigeons wander freely over her bed, chair and dresser. The management has not repaired the window or lock for three years and has cited her for—believe it or not—having pets in her room!

Betty managed to survive the Holocaust by being very quiet. She will not ask for help with her housing problems because she believes that will only make things worse. Remaining quiet may have helped Betty survive the Holocaust,

(Cont.)

◆

but it is not a useful tool for a woman in danger of eviction. The landlord places psychological and physical pressure on Betty and other hotel residents to move. He takes forever to fix a faucet or offers a few thousand dollars incentive to encourage the tenant to relocate.

Betty needs a homelessness prevention service—otherwise she will probably lose her apartment and face a high risk of being homeless. This is where Dorot, a Jewish service agency, and its Homelessness Prevention Service enters the picture, providing counseling and, where needed, transitional housing in its fourteen-bed site on West 95th Street in Manhattan.

The day I visited, seven men and three women were receiving help in obtaining benefits, professional counseling, a clean room and two meals a day. One of them was Saul, a sixty-four-year-old writer, who had lived all his life on the Upper West Side. Gentrification had pushed him out of his apartment and forced him to move to Michigan to live with his sister. Treated there for depression, he returned to Manhattan to be closer to friends.

Dorot's case worker had spent many hours with Saul, evaluating his benefits, helping him fill out forms and dispatching him to City Hall to get his monthly checks flowing. Upon arrival, he learned that the city clerks had "lost" his papers between the second and third floors.

Dorot helped him recover his benefits and obtain a permanent room in a nearby SRO hotel. He enjoys sports, knows how to dress and receives packages from Dorot on every Jewish holiday. The day I saw Saul, he was happier than he had been in a long time.

Tenants like Betty and Saul, who get pushed around very easily, desperately need an effective advocate. They need empowerment.

Tenant Empowerment

Tenants who live in large-scale developments must be organized or events can quickly overtake them. In the mid-1980s, 4,300 low-income housing units in Boston were in deep financial trouble. 2,300 of them were for sale to speculators. The tenants were like pawns in a real-life game of Monopoly. Eviction – which was imminent – would have meant disaster for perhaps 10,000 men, women and children. The tenants of Boston's Castle Square Apartments avoided disaster because they turned to the Boston HUD Tenants' Alliance.

Alone the residents were impotent; united they had power. With "tenant empowerment," low-income renters have the tools to achieve just about anything.

In April 1990, the Castle Square group negotiated what experts described as

> a remarkable tenant buyout agreement – remarkable because it was negotiated with the for-profit seller and buyer *after* the sale had been completed. And remarkable because the tenants got the seller and buyer to set aside $2.7 million from the sale to form a Tenant Equity and Repair Fund that the tenants can use in twelve years to purchase and repair the building.[5]

The Alliance involved the tenants at every step of the negotiations, even translating all discussions into Chinese so every tenant could participate. By 1990, the Alliance had helped 3,500 families successfully fight eviction and win physical and economic improvements.

Tenants were faced with a different kind of challenge at 46 North Parkside in Chicago. The utilities had been cut off. The heat was shut down. No one in the building could take a bath or cook a meal. Augusta Caldwell shivered all day and wondered if, in her old age, she was going to freeze to death.

With property taxes in arrears, the building in chaos, the absentee landlord missing, drug dealers and rats everywhere, you had the perfect recipe for the death of a building and homelessness for twenty-one more families.

Why didn't 46 North Parkside self-destruct? Because the tenants approached the South Austin Coalition Community Council for help in organizing a cooperative corporation.

Each tenant paid $100 to become a shareholder in the corporation that bought the building from the county, renovated it and then established tough rules to keep out drug dealers and squatters.

"I got old fighting for this place," said Ms. Caldwell, who lived there for seventeen years and has never owned anything larger than a television set in her life. "My bones got old in there and everything aches, but I'll do the best I can to make this place work. This is my home. I own it now."[6]

Nina Travis, one of the shareholders in the cooperative, had something to rejoice about. "We are becoming middle class in the middle of the ghetto," she declared, "and I'm proud. I was born in Tennessee. My mama had fourteen children and took in laundry since I was a child. I always dreamed someday of being a lady. At forty-four years old, I own property. I'm a lady now."

Tenant empowerment builds pride and self-esteem. As John McKnight of the Center for Urban Affairs at Northwestern University has observed,

> People are not likely to be organized or empowered on the basis of their needs and deficiencies. An organizer does not go in and say, "It is because you have dropped out of school, are illiterate and have pregnant teenage daughters that I am going to organize you."
>
> An organizer says, "Friend, I see in you—me. I see your capacities." And it is peculiarly in associations and be-

tween friends that capacities are understood and from professions that deficiencies are seen. . . .

"No longer do I call you servants, for the servant does not know what his master is doing. But I have called you friends."[7]

Either You Plan or They Plan For You

Cochran Gardens is a St. Louis public housing project with flower lined paths, children's play equipment and freshly painted safe hallways. It wasn't always that way. Not so long ago, graffiti, broken windows and shootings plagued Cochran.

How did such a transformation take place? Much of it because of Bertha Gilkey. She grew up in the project and at age 20 was elected head of the tenants' association.

She motivated residents of each floor to paint their hallways. How? "If you don't paint your hall, it won't get done." Children who saw their friend's hall painted pressured their parents to do the same.

Bertha asked the residents what they wanted most. They replied, "A laundromat that works!" Previous ones had been vandalized. Improvement through empowerment–and it worked! A tenants' committee patrol ended fights in the project, deposited garbage properly and protected the laundromat. In school students wrote papers on "What I Like About Living in Cochran Gardens" and kids in art class built a model of the project.

Like Chicago's 46 North Parkside, Cochran's tenants today own and manage the development. It includes town houses, a day-care center, health clinic, a vocational training program and even a catering service.

Bertha Gilkey has become a national heroine, and Cochran Gardens a model of how to build pride. She captured the spirit of her effort with eight words: "Either you plan or they plan for you."[8]

The State of New Jersey Rescued 15,000 at Low Cost

The State of New Jersey has one of the best homelessness prevention programs in the nation. Its purpose: to provide "temporary assistance of last resort (loans, security, etc.) to households facing imminent eviction or foreclosure because they lack adequate funds *for reasons beyond their control* (italics mine)." The urgent need might be the result of a medical crisis, a natural disaster, nonpayment of child support, job loss or a delay in receiving government benefits.

Over a period of only two-and-a-half years ending June 1987, here are the stunning results:

> Six-thousand households (15,000 persons) avoided home-lessness at an average cost of $1,000 (on a total expenditure of about $6.5 million). Preliminary evaluations have shown:
>
> 1. the program has a two-thirds success rate;
> 2. the program is two to three times more cost effective than shelters;
> 3. the program is ten to twenty times more cost effective than the use of welfare motels.[9]

The Homelessness Prevention Program revealed one of the main causes of homelessness is delay in government benefit payments. If an unemployment, disability or supplemental social security benefit does not arrive for one to six months (as is often the case), a family living on the "knife-edge" of poverty cannot continue to make rent payments. The result will be homelessness at great financial and human cost to them and to the public.

What does it take for a state to have an effective, low-cost prevention program? It takes some enlightened advocates and a few thousand people in and out of government who are convinced that homelessness is a problem that can be solved.

The men and women who build Habitat homes are average

citizens, like you and me. After obtaining financing, they paint, hammer, saw and trim, producing housing in the right places at the right time.

The people who establish shelters in churches and synagogues and centers for homelessness prevention are the ones we sit next to on Friday nights or Sunday mornings.

There are no miracles here, no revelations from on high. Only a sense that for this kind of work we have been put on Earth – to improve the lives of those less fortunate than we.

10

HOUSING: WHOSE JOB IS IT?

Nearly everyone agrees: unless we build more clean, secure low-income housing, growing numbers of homeless will live on the streets and under the bridges of our nation. In a forty-six-city survey by the Partnership for the Homeless, sixty percent of those surveyed responded that the lack of decent and affordable housing for low-income households was the principal cause of homelessness in their area.[1]

How did we get ourselves into this predicament?

According to experts, the main culprits are:

1. **The Government**
   During the Reagan Administration, federal funds for housing plummeted from $31 billion annually (1979) to $6.9 billion (1989). Cuts in housing were greater than in any other federal program.

2. **Urban Renewal**
   Over four million units that were affordable to low-income families have been lost since 1975, due mostly to decay and demolition. Between 1970 and 1982, the United States lost

115

fifty percent of its single room occupancy units because of urban renewal, land clearance and tax-advantaged gentrification.[2]

3. **Inflation**
Housing costs – for owners and renters – have skyrocketed in the past decade. Low-income wages have not kept pace. The cheapest one-bedroom apartment in Atlanta in 1987 rented for $304. In Los Angeles, a two-bedroom unit in a lower socioeconomic area was $490. Minimum-wage workers then took home about $500 a month. Not much left over for food or clothing![3]

4. **Unemployment and Economic Dislocation**
The homeless are not necessarily "chronically unemployable." Many of them held jobs and became unemployed because of economic dislocation. In the 1980s, one out of every eight American workers experienced dislocation. Some became homeless.

A Rental
Housing Crisis

America is in the midst of a rental housing crisis. During the 1980s, almost no new rental housing was erected in New Jersey. In California, the District of Columbia and Nevada as well as New Jersey, there were three times as many low-income renters as housing units in their price range. In California alone the shortage of such units in 1989 was an astounding 789,406. Nationally, the shortfall is nearly four million. A recent MIT study predicted that, if present trends in federal housing policy continue, the low-rent housing gap will swell to seven million units by the end of the 1990s.[4]

Most major American cities have such enormous unmet demands for low-income housing that they have closed their waiting lists. Imagine looking for a two-bedroom subsidized apartment in New York or Chicago and being told that you will have to wait ten to eleven years.[5]

We are all familiar with long-term sentences for heinous crimes. But how many of us can conceive what it is like to be told that it may be eleven years before decent housing is available? For some that means being condemned to shelters, hovels or drug- and crime-infested streets for a substantial portion of your natural life. It is a sentence handed down not by a judge in court, but by the federal government, urban renewal programs, inflation and escalating unemployment.

Whose Job Is It?

The question is: whose job is it to build affordable dwellings?

Some argue that the task is so massive that *only* the government is capable of that mission.

Others maintain the opposite: that given the federal deficit, such enormous costs – perhaps as much as $500 billion – could never be borne by the public sector.

It is a big mistake to see this as an either/or question. Without massive government participation – especially on the federal level – the tragedy will deepen. But government by itself cannot do the job. Community involvement is indispensable; without neighborhood participation, crime, drugs, unemployment and family disintegration are inevitable.

Let's first consider what the government has and has not done.

In the middle of 1987, Congress enacted the Stewart B. McKinney Homeless Assistance Act, named after the Connecticut Republican congressman who died shortly before its passage. President Reagan, who believed that most homeless people "choose" that condition for themselves, signed the bill at

117

night. A White House aide explained that Reagan took that unusual step to convey his "lack of enthusiasm."

While the McKinney Act authorized funding for some twenty different programs at $615-$634 million in 1988-1989, barely half that amount was actually spent. Most of the programs support shelters, job training, health care or alcohol and drug abuse treatment. The bureaucratic obstacles were daunting. Some of the applications for the money were sixty-six pages long! In one instance, a New York City shelter was awarded $11,500 of McKinney money for a new boiler. It took fifteen months for the check to arrive.

On the other hand, some shelters, day-care centers and the like could not have made it without McKinney funds. But even the amounts authorized were wholly inadequate to the national task. Moreover, McKinney provided almost no funds for low-income housing.

> ◆ *Bob Nasdor wanted to build homes for thirty homeless families on three empty acres in Montclair, New Jersey, where a military golf course had stood decades before. The McKinney Act authorized the use of "underutilized federal property for the homeless." When Nasdor applied to the government for the land, he was told that it was "excess" rather than "underutilized"–so it was not available. It took Oliver Gasch, a Federal District Court Judge in Washington, D.C., to order the government to stop playing*
> ◆ *semantic games and turn over the land.*[6]

In 1983, Congress established the Emergency Food and Shelter National Board to assist non-profit groups with shelters, soup kitchens, feeding programs and emergency one-month rent and utility payments. But the program, which disbursed $603 million in its first five years through religious groups, was a drop in the bucket. It was never intended to address the long-term housing needs of the homeless.[7]

On the Other Hand:
Some Achievements

As the decade of the 1990s was aborning, there were signs of concern about the homelessness situation at the federal level. In 1989, after a three-hour meeting with organizers of the Housing Now March, HUD Secretary Jack Kemp signed a letter of understanding committing the Bush Administration to action. They will make ten percent of the single-family homes in HUD's inventory available to the homeless. That comes to 5,000 units. Assuming four to a family, that pledge, if fulfilled, might house 20,000 souls, perhaps one percent of the nation's homeless. Not much—but with ninety-nine similar programs, the job might get done.[8]

The year 1990 saw the passage of the most far-reaching housing legislation since 1974: the Cranston-Gonzalez National Affordable Housing Act. As a result of this act, low-income people received $9.5 billion in fiscal year 1991, a significant increase over previous years.

Here are some of the highlights of this landmark legislation:

- HOUSING GRANTS: In 1991-1992 $3.1 billion was be awarded to state and local governments to produce, acquire and renovate housing, primarily for low- and moderate-income people. It specifically promotes community-based non-profit housing development.

- COMMUNITY DEVELOPMENT BLOCK GRANTS: Community-based non-profit corporations will have access to $6.44 billion to build housing for low- and moderate-income families.

- HOPE FUNDS: Tenants will have this assistance in purchasing federally-assisted public housing properties.

119

- PRESERVATION OF LOW-INCOME UNITS: This is a permanent solution to the looming prepayment crisis. Owners of subsidized housing would have been able to pay off federally-subsidized mortgages, raise the rents on 900,000 units and evict low-income tenants. Now they must keep their units affordable or sell the property to a buyer who will.

- NEW CONSTRUCTION: For the first time since the 1970s, funding will be set aside specifically for new construction.

- SPECIAL NEEDS: Modest appropriations for groups with special needs such as Native Americans, elderly and those with AIDS, will available.

We Subsidize Housing for the Prosperous

This pivotal legislation was a long time in coming and it will take some years before its impact is fully felt. In the meantime, countless men, women and children have endured enormous pain and will continue to suffer. Without the efforts of a determined corps of advocates as described in chapter eleven, the Housing Act would have been unthinkable.

Most of us forget that Washington, D.C., has been subsidizing middle- and upper-income housing for decades. After the Great Depression and World War II, the nation's housing stock was severely retarded. The young families who gave birth to the "baby boomers" needed housing and an attractive environment.

The key was low-cost financing. As families purchased homes – especially in the suburbs – FHA insurance and VA guarantees stood behind the mortgages. This reduced the risk of loss for banks, and Savings and Loan organizations (S&Ls) made lower interest rates and long-term payouts possible.

In addition, homeowners have been able to take deductions on their income tax for mortgage interest and property taxes. In 1988 the cost of these deductions in foregone federal revenue was $50 billion. Most of those deductions went to the eleven percent of the population earning over $50,000 a year. Two percent went to those earning less than $20,000.

Those deductions may well be in the public interest. But don't those who are receiving them – and that is probably most of us reading this book – have a responsibility to insure that more federal funds are spent for low-income housing?

If you are convinced that the federal government should be doing more than it is and if you are prepared to be an advocate for the homeless and the nearly homeless, what should you demand from your representatives in Washington?[9]

Washington: This Is What We Expect

• Commitment

We must insist that our senators and congresspeople elevate low-income housing to a high priority on their legislative agenda and that the President provide moral leadership. Without such a commitment, dramatic progress is inconceivable.

• Funding

Transformations in the former USSR and Eastern Europe offer an opportunity for significant reductions in defense spending by the United States. Some of this "peace dividend" must be redirected to make up for the $25 billion per year which has been cut from the housing budget since 1979. Appeals for military spending must not be allowed to undermine funding for the needy.

• Rent Subsidies

The government's "affordability" standard dictates that poor households should pay no more than thirty percent of their income for rent. Yet, even with housing vouchers, over half of low-income renters are paying sixty percent or more of their income for housing. Project-based subsidies should be reinstituted and funding for rent subsidies increased.

- **New Partnerships**
The federal government should provide greater tax incentives for private developers to build low-income housing. It should encourage churches, synagogues and nonprofit community groups to establish creative partnerships to build and preserve affordable housing.

- **New Forms of Ownership**
The federal government should encourage new forms of ownership, such as "social ownership" or "mutual housing." Under such arrangements, tenants' organizations, community groups or government entities own property for the benefit of residents.

- **Rural Housing and Native Americans**
Rural and Native American communities are less visible, yet they contain forty percent of the nation's homeless. Urban and suburban residents should insist that those needs be addressed.

- **Cutting the Red Tape**
HUD regulations need to be simplified. HUD personnel must demonstrate greater flexibility and sensitivity to special local and regional needs.

- **Enforcement of Fair Housing Laws**
Blacks and other minorities still have difficulty renting or purchasing homes in many neighborhoods and buildings. Non-discrimination in housing must be vigorously enforced.

One Answer:
Creative Partnerships

One answer to the housing crisis is a network of creative partnerships between government agencies (federal, state and local), not-for-profit agencies and private companies.

Here's how it worked successfully in Milwaukee. In 1986, ten corporate and individual lenders teamed up with the city of Milwaukee and the Wisconsin Electric Power company to create the Housing Partnership Corporation (HPC). With a $12 million commitment, they joined with the Westside Conservation Corporation, a neighborhood-based low-income housing developer, to purchase and rehabilitate a twenty-six-unit apartment building.

HPC was able to raise additional money at 4.5 percent interest through a combination of city bond monies available at two percent and private lenders' capital at seven percent.

With the help of the First Bank of Milwaukee, HPC purchased the building for $75,000, although it was worth $200,000. The $125,000 difference was considered a contribution to the Westside Conservation Corporation. Architectural services were donated by local colleges; the building industry provided goods and services and the Wisconsin Housing and Economic Development Corporation made a $48,000 grant.

Total development costs came to $200,000-$350,000, with one-bedroom units renting for $300 and studios at $180.

In four years, HPC has facilitated the purchase and rehabilitation of 175 units with plans for many more, all in partnership with neighborhood associations.[10]

> ◆ *Ask your community to try this idea on for size: the Housing Trust Fund. These are dedicated sources of revenue for the purpose of providing low- and moderate-income housing.*
> ◆ (Cont.)

> *Where does the money come from? The possibilities vary: a tax on real estate sales, interest on real estate escrow accounts and required contributions from developers of office buildings.*
>
> *As of 1989, there were thirty-four Housing Trust Funds in the United States with fifteen more under development. Most provide about $1.5 million each to produce or improve housing, and five have committed over $20 million each.*
>
> *It is a possibility to explore with your city's leadership.*[11]

The Church:
Often the Only Institution Left

When neighborhoods deteriorate, the church is often the most significant institution left. When religious institutions create a partnership with people involved in renewal, amazing things can happen.

Many city officials and housing activists are learning from the nonprofit Nehemiah Plan. In East Brooklyn a group of attached houses has become a housing success story and a model for federal legislation. More than 1,000 of the Brooklyn homes have been sold to families of moderate incomes for $41,000 each. Eight out of ten families moving in to Nehemiah homes came from public or subsidized housing. Thousands more units are on the drawing boards.

Nehemiah began when five pastors from Brooklyn churches—Roman Catholic, Baptist and Lutheran—created the East Brooklyn Churches Organization, a coalition of fifty-two local organizations with more than 30,000 members.

The churches created an $8 million financing pool, with $1 million each from the Lutheran Church (Missouri Synod) and the Episcopal Diocese of Long Island and $3 million from the Catholic Diocese of Brooklyn.[12]

In 1968, North Philadelphia looked like a war zone. Today, while pockets of decay still pervade the ghetto, there are pleasant surprises – twenty-three new solar townhouses and 200 other units of renovated housing. Four hundred parcels are "land banked" for future use, including the start of commercial development along Columbia Avenue. This transformation was sparked by the congregants of the National Temple Baptist Church and the nonprofit corporation they created in 1968. Their partners? community development block grants, city funds, American Express, the Catholic Church, Ford Foundation, Pew Trust, Mellon Bank and the Local Initiatives Support Corporation. An impressive, no-nonsense partnership.[13]

A 1988 survey revealed that over 2,000 community-based organizations were in the low-income housing business. Those participating in the survey had built or restored 125,000 units through 1987 and, by 1990, 250,000 or more. Quite a contribution to the housing crisis.

These community-based enterprises accounted for the creation or retention of 90,000 jobs in 1984-1989. Major support is now forthcoming from Lilly Endowment and the Ford Foundation.[14] The key elements are a caring community, good organization and leverage. With leverage, relatively small amounts of seed money ($10,000-$20,000) can generate ten to fifty times that sum from government, banks and corporations.

What about areas that have become emblematic of the worst housing conditions in our nation – like the South Bronx in New York City? Can even those "disaster areas" be helped by such partnerships?

Charlene Moats traced the cycle of devastation and renewal that has changed the face of her South Bronx neighborhood. "I've been here thirty years," she told a reporter, "and I remember when this whole block was abandoned." Today, every building on the block is either renovated or undergoing reconstruction.[15]

How did it happen that parts of the South Bronx–which most New Yorkers had given up on–now has a bright future? A major reason is community groups like Banana Kelly and Build. They are among the dozens of local nonprofits that have used a combination of federal tax credits and city and state assistance to create housing miracles.

How does the Low Income Tax Credit program work? The federal government assigns tax credits to each state. The state housing authority then passes these tax credits on to private developers who build low-cost housing. According to the Topsfield Foundation, these credits may be the single most effective stimulus for the construction of low cost housing today.[16] A company that invests $1 million in a financing pool for low-income housing could realize $2.3 million in tax savings over fifteen years.[17]

Fortune 500 Companies
Join the Battle

If a company invests $1 million in a financing pool for low-income housing, over the course of fifteen years it could realize $2.3 million in tax savings. The Federal National Mortgage Association (Fannie Mae), the world's largest private mortgage lender, has made $60 million available through the use of the tax credit. But most companies are not involved in the homeless issue, not as participants in financial pools nor even as sponsors of child- and elder-care programs.

As is true of all the methods described in this chapter, corporate participation alone will not solve the low-income housing crisis. But it can make a visible dent in the armor of homelessness. Hundreds of thousands of units can be built or restored using this technique–if the will to do it exists.

In the 1980s, the Enterprise Foundation, established by developer James W. Rouse, enabled groups like Banana Kelly,

Build and dozens more to finance some of their projects with federal tax credits.[18] Enterprise, the Local Initiatives Support Corporation and many other nonprofit groups are linking developers and investors, including many Fortune 500 companies.[19]

◆ *James Rouse credits the congregants of the Church of the Savior in Washington, D.C., as his inspiration for establishing the Enterprise Foundation. In 1973, they approached him for assistance in rehabilitating two dilapidated apartment buildings. . . . Rouse first tried to steer them to government programs, but finally, impressed with their commitment and determination, he agreed to personally finance the buildings' $625,000 purchase price.*

Rouse recalls the first visit to "his" apartments: "The stench was so terrible I gagged. Garbage and rubbish were piled on stairwells and elevator shaft. . . . There were 947 housing-code violations. It was just a pesthole—but fully occupied."

To do the work, the congregants formed Jubilee Housing, which mobilized neighborhood residents to contribute some 50,000 hours of "sweat equity." Jubilee subsequently became the flagship of the Enterprise Foundation net-
◆ *work.* [20]

"The not-for-profits bring something that dollars and cents can't measure," said Felice Michetti, New York City's Acting Commissioner of Housing Preservation and Development. "They know neighborhoods as no private developer could know them. They look at tenants as neighborhood residents. There's a difference between a tenant and a neighborhood resident."

127

Under Banana Kelly's guidance, the residents of one building took control of their own lives. The first families to reside in a building often determine how the remaining families will be selected. At one of the residents' meetings, a proposal was made that the new families who come from shelters and welfare hotels prove that they have in the past maintained apartments. "Can we be sure that someone who's only lived in a hotel or shelter or their parents' house is responsible?" a resident asked.

A fellow resident quickly reminded them that all those in the room had themselves been homeless just a few months before. "We can set an example," she said. "Just because you come from nowhere doesn't mean you're going nowhere."

As many as 45,000 people still live in single-room-occupancy hotels (SROs) in New York City alone. Tens of thousands more called them home before the hotels were renovated or demolished to make room for luxury apartments or commercial space. Los Angeles, Chicago and other major cities have also lost SROs at a rapid rate.

Most of us think of the SRO as a dilapidated, drug-ridden, vermin-infested cell with no redeeming qualities. But as demonstrated by the Church and Temple Program on Los Angeles's skid row,[21] as well as in San Diego and New York's Upper West Side, clean, secure, drug-free, affordable housing can emerge from cooperative efforts of the public and nonprofit sectors.

Full Service Housing—
Even Little League

We have surveyed a number of public and private sector partnerships that have transformed the face of neighborhoods in distress. But they are effective only to the extent that they serve the whole person. A room, an apartment or a home is not enough unless there are also food, counseling, employment, medical care and education. It is a myth to believe that all a pregnant, crack-addicted teenage prostitute with AIDS needs is a place to call home. Linkage is the way to go. Housing advocates must weave a web of services.[22]

Consider the efforts of Andrew Cuomo, son of the New York governor. He combined land donated by New York City, construction paid for by tax-exempt state bonds and pro bono legal and architectural services. The result: 200 units of transitional housing in Brooklyn. The bonds will be paid off with funds that city agencies pay Cuomo's group, H.E.L.P. (Housing Enterprise for the Less Privileged), to house the families. It is a fraction of what the city would pay for dingy welfare hotels.

But Cuomo and his not-for-profit organization, H.E.L.P., did more than just hand over apartment keys to families in need. They brought in the Red Cross to operate a facility with on-site professionals providing drug and alcohol counseling, vocational guidance, medical service, day care and parenting instruction.

The need for such services was illustrated one day when Cuomo was observing Little League tryouts at the facility. He noticed a young boy of ten or eleven extending his glove to catch a ball. Yet over and over, the ball hit him in the chest.

When he came up to bat, the boy took his swing only after the ball hit the catcher's mitt. This happened again and again.

Cuomo brought the youngster to the health center where a test determined that he was legally blind. How was it possible, demanded Cuomo, that this could have gone undetected for so long? How could he have managed his school work?

The answer to Cuomo's question came quickly: he had never been to school.[23]

H.E.L.P. builds more than housing units; it rebuilds lives by building full-service communities – in Brooklyn, the South Bronx, Albany and Westchester County. (Westchester, one of America's most affluent counties, has over 5,000 homeless people.)

The accomplishments of religious organizations and

community-based groups, as well as nonprofit and for-profit builders, have been extraordinary. Because of these achievements, there is a temptation to release federal, state and local governments from their responsibilities. That would be a calamity. The task is far too great for voluntary groups to go it alone; they could never muster the resources required to do the job. Government has a responsibility to the poor of our land.

Government should encourage – with tax incentives, well-focused subsidies and capital grants – the Banana Kellys and the Andrew Cuomos of our land. Together with massive doses of well-directed government assistance, the problem can be solved.

Who will make that happen? Ultimately the buck stops with you and me, the consumers and the voters of this nation. We have no one but ourselves to thank for our successes, such as the National Affordable Housing Act, or to blame for our failures, the homeless that populate our streets and shelters.

11
WHO WILL SPEAK
FOR THE HOMELESS?

◆————————————————————————————————◆

The habit of inattention must be considered the greatest
defect of the democratic character.

Alexis de Tocqueville[1]

C ongress responds to the will of the voters. But our homeless citizens rarely vote. And with a few dramatic excep-
tions, they neither write nor visit their congressperson or senator. When is the last time that you wrote your representative? If
neither you nor I will lobby the halls of Congress for the homeless, who will speak for them? Who will be their advocates?

To understand the potential number of advocates for the
homeless in this nation, consider just one modest operation, the
Interfaith Hospitality Networks. Since the first network was
founded by Karen Olson in Central New Jersey in 1985, it has
expanded to twenty-two networks in six states. Over 22,000
volunteers from hundreds of churches and synagogues are involved. All from just one modest-size network!

Now estimate the number of men, women and children
throughout the country who voluntarily staff shelters, serve
meals and counsel. At least a half million and possibly many

131

times that figure. Consider this: *if only ten percent of those volunteers—say 50,000—were to become vocal advocates for the homeless, what a difference they would make.*

Ten Letters Can Change the World

Our representatives rarely receive more than three visits or ten letters about any subject. When the numbers exceed that amount, they sit up and take note. Personal visits are the most potent. Letters are next; telephone calls are third best.

There are 535 senators and representatives in the United States Congress. It would take only 53,500 citizens from this vast nation to average 100 communications to each federal legislator—that is 1,070 per state, an easily reachable number. (Many individual churches and synagogues have that many adult members alone.) What an overwhelming impact they would have.

> ◆ *Real political issues cannot be manufactured by the leaders of political parties. The real political issues of the day declare themselves and come out of the depths of that deep which we call public opinion.*
> ◆ President James A. Garfield

How Much Do We Care?

Just how much do Americans care and how much are we willing to sacrifice?

When it comes to personal sacrifice, we are schizophrenic. On the one hand, most of us feel generous toward our fellow human beings. When called upon to help, we often respond with a full heart. I once knew a rather nasty person with whom it was difficult to communicate. When I finally did, I asked myself why I had bothered. He never had a kind word for me or anyone else.

One day our synagogue needed help with a tutorial program in a low-income area. Someone recruited him. The day after his first tutorial, he sat in my office transformed into a nicer person, amazed that he had never appreciated life as much as when he helped a ten year-old with simple arithmetic.

On the other hand, how often do we sacrifice for someone in need? Review the past year of your life. How often did you? We speak glibly about helping others, and we can all think of some dramatic, even courageous examples, but in reality, most of us do very little for others besides our immediate family.

We must start by taking a look at our own attitude. The first century Hebrew sage, Hillel, taught us:

> If I am not for myself,
> Who will be for me?
> But if I am only for myself,
> What am I?
> And if not now, when?

Certainly we all need to start with ourselves. Unless we take care of our own needs and those of our family who depend upon us, we will not be able to be of much help to others. But a life that ends with us has little depth and is ultimately unfulfilling.

As the homeless grow in number, we ought to be asking ourselves some questions about how we fit into the desperate scheme of things.

- What do we as individuals owe the homeless?

- What does society owe them?

133

• What do our Jewish and Christian roots teach us about the stranger, the homeless, the victim?

• We all enjoy benefits that we have not necessarily earned ourselves and that far exceed what we need to live well. What is our responsibility to share some of those resources? How much and under what conditions?

Faith Ryder, a seventh-grader at St. Joseph's School in New York City, answered the last question well:

> It's awful to think there are people out there who live that way when we just go around and buy meaningless things like magazines or toys or jewelry, 'cause you don't need that stuff.[3]

Is Our Gain
Their Loss?

Many of us live in homes or apartments that we have owned for over ten years. Or we may have recently sold a residence. In either case, millions of Americans have benefited financially from the dramatic escalation of housing values in the 1980s. Their assets—at least on paper—have swelled as inflation and market pressures have pushed up property values.

But those same market pressures have squeezed millions of low-income families out of the market altogether. Not only can they not afford to buy, they cannot even afford to rent. As for those of us who do live in homes and condominiums that have escalated in value, what is our obligation to the homeless?

In 1988, sixty percent of Americans thought that federal spending for the homeless should be increased and nearly all of those were willing to pay more taxes for that purpose. In February 1990 seventy-six percent believed that the problem of the homeless would either worsen or remain the same.[4]

The majority of Americans know that we have a growing problem *and* are willing to do something about it.

Raising the Roof
with Legislators

Jerald Scott, who oversees human welfare issues for the United Methodist Church, put it bluntly: "We must tell our representatives that if they do not make low-income housing their priority, we are not going to send them back to Washington." According to Scott, Housing Now's October 1989 March on Washington was impressive, but it was also a hit-and-run operation. Once the marchers went back to their communities, a relative quiet resumed on the housing front and many legislators felt free of pressure.

That is why in January 1990 religious-sponsored social justice groups brought several hundred women and men together in Washington, D.C., for a conference titled, "Raising the Roof." These were professional and volunteer housing activists working in the religious community. Meeting at round tables with congresspersons and their aides, they discussed proposed housing legislation and how it would impact on their work.

Most of the legislators and their aides had never before heard from religiously-motivated people who work the streets and shelters. Not only were they impressed by the step-by-step evaluation of housing legislation, but they also learned that many of their constituents care about this issue out of deep religious commitment. Since the conference, those advocates have lobbied, and when they did, they packed a bigger wallop than ever before. Every person who left that conference and reached out to her congressperson or senator contributed to the passage of the landmark National Affordable Housing Act of 1990.[5]

What ◆ *Make policy. Let's face it. Housing is not as*
Can *"sexy" as a lot of other issues, but it matters. It*
One *matters a lot, and if you want to influence hous-*
Person Do? *ing policy, great. Since the housing issue does not*
come up that often, your elected officials will lis-
ten when you bring it up, particularly if you are
not a housing advocate whose job depends on
increased funding or a tenant trying to hold onto
his or her home. So let our local, state and federal
representatives know that you are concerned
about housing and are willing to support decent
◆ *programs. And keep letting them know.*[6]

Every Volunteer –
a Potential Advocate

Every volunteer who works with the homeless is a potential
advocate. Working in a shelter and serving food are important.
But if that is all we do, we shall fail. Our goal is to move people
out of shelters and soup kitchens into transitional and permanent housing with employment counseling and medical care.
For that, we must be resolute advocates.

If you want to talk about big numbers, every church and
synagogue member is a potential supporter of the homeless.
How can you, as a local volunteer, become an effective advocate?

- By recognizing that your work with the homeless has
not only educated you, but that it has *empowered* you to
speak with authority. After providing direct service to the
homeless, you know more about what is needed than
most citizens. You can help people who make policy
decisions see the homeless problem in human terms.
- By understanding that shelters and soup kitchens are
"band-aid" treatments. They relieve the immediate crisis,
but do not solve the problem. In some ways, they mask
the illness, giving the impression that the patient is being

treated, while in reality he is getting worse. To be effective, volunteers must become advocates of affordable housing and job training, health care, inner city education and support services for the homeless.

• By making a powerful impact on our senators and representatives with letters urging more funds and tax incentives for affordable housing and by consistent visits to their district and Washington offices.

• By letters to the editor, articles in local papers and paid advertisements which shape public opinion.

• By pressing housing issues at election time, by obtaining commitments at candidate forums and by personal visits with the office-seeker. Fund-raising events present particularly effective moments for educating the candidates.

• By enlisting social justice committees and entire memberships of synagogues and churches for the cause. It is an excellent way of getting inactive members involved in programs and in touch with their own spirituality. Religious feelings quickly surface when we work with the homeless. It is a rare opportunity to confront our own humanity.

It is easy to become discouraged when the problem is so enormous and we feel so inadequate. When I start to feel that way, I remember the story of Rabbi Israel Salanter, who was once walking in the rain. He felt his feet getting wet because his soles needed repairing. He stepped into a cobbler's shop to have them mended, but noticed that the cobbler's candle was down to one-eighth of an inch.

Knowing that the cobbler needed the light of the candle to walk home, Rabbi Salanter volunteered to come back another day. But the cobbler insisted on doing the work and said, "My father taught me that as long as there is a little candlelight left, there is still time to mend."

Let's not put it off to another day. We need strong advocates who insist that there is still time to mend.

12
WHERE DO WE GO FROM HERE?

> You are not required to complete the task.
> But neither are you at liberty to abstain
> from it altogether.
>
> Rabbi Tarfon[1]

Can we overcome the housing crisis that confronts low-income people? Can we provide decent housing for the men, women and children who call the streets and shelters their home?

The answer is yes, but only if. . .

We launch a broad scale attack on the root causes of unemployment and on jobs that pay poverty-level wages. Forty-four percent of all the new jobs created between 1982 and 1988 were at poverty-level wages.[2]

The rich are growing richer and the poor are becoming poorer. Inequity in pay grew in the eighties at an alarming rate, while tax subsidies for the wealthy continued at high levels.

Yes, we can provide housing for the homeless if we recognize that building shelters is a stop gap measure, like putting pots in the living room to catch dripping water without fixing the roof.[3]

The answer is permanent low-cost housing built by partnerships of government, business, not-for-profit community development corporations, foundations, neighborhood agencies, churches and synagogues. Costs must be controlled, profits limited and units made available on a non-discriminatory basis. Tenants do best when they are empowered and have a stake in their home and their future.

In the end, the question is: do we see the poor as ne'er-do-wells taking advantage of a generous people—or as unfortunate victims of a competitive system for which they are not trained? If the answer is the former, then we must tell our children, our grandchildren and ourselves that we will be stepping over the bodies of growing numbers of homeless on the streets of North America for the rest of our lives. But if the answer is the latter, then we have an opportunity to leave a rich legacy of justice and compassion to the next generation.

Which will it be? Our religious traditions—Christian and Jewish alike—are indisputably clear: the homeless and the poor need to be their partners. We are obligated to undertake imaginative efforts with them to eradicate homelessness from our land.

Each of the creative and successful programs described in this volume reaches only a fraction of the nation's homeless. But one by one by one, each effort added to another, will eventually transform our cities, suburbs and rural communities into a society that we shall be proud of.

Let it be said by generations to come that we saw the homeless in our land and that we did not turn away.

FORTY THINGS
EVERYONE CAN DO
TO HELP THE HOMELESS

1. Learn about the homeless
2. Respect the homeless as individuals
3. When confronted by the homeless respond with kindness
4. Carry fast-food gift certificates
5. Develop lists of shelters
6. Give money (change on the street, charity to social service agencies, etc.)
7. Give recyclables
8. Give proceeds from a craft sale
9. Give clothing
10. Give a bag of groceries
11. Give toys
12. Give welcome kits for new residents (paper goods, dishes, etc.)
13. Give a portion of what you'd spend on a party
14. Volunteer to help the homeless at a shelter or a soup kitchen
15. Volunteer your professional talents
16. Volunteer your hobbies
17. Volunteer to tutor homeless children

18. Volunteer to take homeless children on trips
19. Volunteer job training
20. Volunteer to organize a thrift shop
21. Volunteer at battered women's shelters
22. Teach others about the homeless
23. Publish shelter information in community newspapers
24. Enlist community organizations as advocates
25. Educate your children about the homeless
26. Sign up your company/school for fundraising events
27. Ask your clergy, church or synagogue to help

What Children Can Do

28. Teach their friends
29. Donate toys and games
30. Collect charity at school
31. Donate admissions to a school event
32. Play with children in a shelter

If You Can Really Make a Commitment

33. Employ the homeless
34. Join Habitat for Humanity to help build houses for families in danger of becoming homeless
35. Form a transitional housing program to help find affordable housing for those in danger of eviction
36. Solicit funding from corporations
37. Assist the homeless to apply for governmental aid
38. Visit your own government representatives as an advocate on this issue
39. Push for state and non-profit homelessness prevention programs
40. Send us your creative ideas

BIBLIOGRAPHY

Against All Odds: The Achievements of Community-Based Development Organizations (Washington, D.C.: National Congress for Community Economic Development, 1989).

Blau, Joel, *The Visible Poor: Homelessness in the United States* (New York: Oxford University Press, 1992).

Breakey, William R., et al., "Health and Mental Health Problems of Homeless Men and Women in Baltimore," *Journal of the American Medical Association* (Sep. 8, 1989), 1352-1357.

Brooks, Mary E., *A Survey of Housing Trust Funds* (Washington, D.C.: Center for Community Change, 1989).

Building On Faith, Models of Church-Sponsored Affordable Housing Programs in the Washington, D.C. Area (Washington, D.C.: The Churches Conference on Shelter and Housing, 1989).

Choices: A Study Circle on Homelessness and Affordable Housing (Pomfret, CT: Topsfield Foundation, 1990).

The Effects of Subsidized and Affordable Housing on Property Values: A Survey of Research (California: State of California Department of Housing and Community Development, 1988).

Encyclopedia Judaica (Jerusalem: Keter Publishing, 1972).

Graham, W. Fred, *The Constructive Revolutionary* (Atlanta: John Knox Press, 1978).

Gramlich, Ed, *Comprehensive Housing Affordability Strategy, A Citizen's Action Guide* (Washington, DC: Center for Community Change, June 1991).

Hammerskjold, Dag, *Markings* (New York: Knopf, 1965).

Heschel, Abraham J., *The Prophets* (New York: Harper & Row, 1962).

Holub, Margaret, *Jewish Laws Which Address Slum Landlording,* unpublished rabbinic thesis (Hebrew Union College, 1986).

Hombs, Mary Ellen and Snyder, Mitch, *Homelessness in America*, 3rd ed. (Washington, D.C.: Community for Creative Non-Violence, 1986).

Homelessness and Affordable Housing, A Resource Book of Churches, ed. James A. McDaniel (New York: United Church Board for Homeland Ministries, 1989).

Homelessness and Housing: A Human Tragedy, A Moral Challenge, 3rd ed. (Washington, D.C.: United States Catholic Conference, 1988).

Homewords (Washington, D.C.: Homelessness Information Exchange).

143

Housing/Shelter, A Background Paper, revised ed. (Pittsburgh: Housing Task Force, Pittsburgh Presbytery, 1988).

Housing: The Third Human Right (Washington, D.C.: United States Catholic Conference, 1985).

Howland, Libby, "Holloway Terrace: Neighborhood Acceptance of Affordable Housing in San Francisco," *Urban Land* (Sep. 1985).

Kahan, Arcadius, "The Early Modern Period," in *The Economic History of the Jews*, ed. Nachum Gross (New York: Schocken, 1975).

Kaplan, Steven, "Women Who Make a Difference," *Family Circle* (Feb. 20, 1990).

Kozol, Jonathan, *Rachel and Her Children, Homeless Families in America* (New York: Fawcett Columbine, 1989).

Krugman, Paul, *The Age of Diminished Expectations* (Cambridge, MA: MIT Press, 1992).

Kushner, Harold, *Who Needs God?* (New York: Summit Books, 1989).

Low Income Housing and Homelessness: Facts and Myths (Washington, D.C.: Low Income Housing Information Service, Jan. 1989).

Maimonides, *The Commandments*, trans. Charles B. Chavel (London: Soncino Press, 1967).

Marcuse, Peter, A study by James Wright and Julie Lam, *Shelterforce* (June/July 1988), 13.

Marin, Peter, "Helping and Hating the Homeless," *Harper's* (Jan. 1987).

McDougall, Diane, "There's No Place Like Home," *World Wide Challenge* (Oct. 1987).

Moving Forward: A National Agenda To Address Homelessness in 1990 and Beyond and a Status Report on Homelessness in America (New York: The Partnership for the Homeless, 1989).

Nauwen, Henri J. M., *Reaching Out* (New York: Doubleday, 1975).

O'Hare, William, "The Eight Myths of Power," *American Demographics* (May 1986).

Peirce, Neal R. and Steinbach, Carol F., *Corrective Capitalism, The Rise of America's Community Development Corporations* (New York: Ford Foundation, 1987).

The Poor Among Us, Jewish Tradition and Social Policy, (New York: The American Jewish Committee, 1986).

Pushed Out: America's Homeless (Washington, D.C.: National Coalition for the Homeless, 1987).

A Rabbinic Anthology, arr. C. G. Montefiore and H. Loewe (Philadelphia: Jewish Publication Society of America, 1960).

Richma, Louis S., "Housing Policy Needs a Rehab," *Fortune* (March 27, 1989), 84-89.

The Right to A Decent Home, A Pastoral Response to the Crisis in Housing (Washington, D.C.: United States Catholic Conference, 1975).

Schwartz, David C. and John H. Glascock, *Combating Homelessness: A Resource Book*, (New Brunswick, NJ: American Affordable Housing Institute, Rutgers Univ.).

A Status Report on Hunger and Homelessness in America's Cities: 1989 and 1990 (Washington, D.C.: The United States Conference of Mayors, Dec. 1989 and Dec. 1990).

Unsworth, Tim, "Shelter Diary: Help Me Make It Through the Night," *U.S. Catholic* (Feb. 1990).

The Way Home, Report of the New York City Commission on the Homeless (New York: City of New York, Feb. 1992).

Yates, Larry, *Low Income Housing in America, An Introduction* (Washington, D.C.: Low Income Housing Information Service, 1990).

NOTES

CHAPTER ONE

[1] The United States Conference of Mayors, *A Status Report on Hunger and Homelessness in America's Cities: 1989* (Dec. 1989), 29. (Referred to hereafter as *Conference of Mayors Report*).

[2] Peter P. Smith, President of the Partnership for the Homeless. Letter to the Editor, *The New York Times* (April 30, 1990).

[3] *Conference of Mayors Report* (Dec. 1989), 9.

[4] *The New York Times* (Feb. 5, 1990).

[5] Mary Ellen Hombs and Mitch Snyder, *Homelessness in America*, 3rd ed. (Washington, D.C.: Community for Creative Non-Violence, 1986), xvii.

[6] Definition of Prof. Gerald T. Hotaling of the Univ. of Lowell, MA, *The New York Times* (Feb. 5, 1990).

[7] *Conference of Mayors Report* (Dec. 1989), 49.

[8] *The New York Times* (April 27, 1990).

[9] Kate Wilson, "An Essay on What It Would Be Like To Be Homeless," *The New York Times* (May 21, 1990).

[10] *Conference of Mayors Report* (Dec. 1989), 44-45.

[11] *Ibid.*, 47.

[12] *Conference of Mayors Report* (Dec. 1990), 39, 50.

[13] *Homelessness and Housing: a Human Tragedy, a Moral Challenge*, 3rd ed. (Washington, D.C.: United States Catholic Conference, 1988), 3.

[14] Craig Rennebohm and Steve Bauck in *Homelessness and Affordable Housing, A Resource Book for Churches*, ed. James A. McDaniel (New York: United Church Board for Homeland Ministries), 33.

[15] William R. Breakey, et al., "Health and Mental Health Problems of Homeless Men and Women in Baltimore," *Journal of the American Medical Association* (Sep. 8, 1989), 1352-1357. A 1992 report by the New York City Commission on the Homeless suggests that 10–12 percent of shelter residents had been hospitalized for a mental problem. *The New York Times*, Feb. 16, 1992.

[16] Jonathan Kozol, *Rachel and Her Children, Homeless Families in America* (New York: Fawcett Columbine, 1989), 135.

[17] Alan Finder, *The New York Times* (Dec. 30, 1990).

[18] These groups overlap. Many who are drug abusers are also in the estimated twenty-five percent who may suffer from severe mental illness. See also 1992 report of the New York City Commission on the Homeless, *The New York Times*, Feb. 16, 1992.

[19] David C. Schwartz and John H. Glasock, *Combating Homelessness: A Resource Book* (New Brunswick, NJ: American Affordable Housing Institute, Rutgers Univ.), 20.

[20] David C. Schwartz, *Combating Homelessness*, 43ff.

[21] *The New York Times* (March 22, 1990); *The New Mexican* (March 22, 1990).

[22] *Albuquerque Journal* (March 22, 1990).

[23] *USA Today* (April 4, 1990).

[24] Felicity Barringer, *The New York Times* (June 11, 1990).

[25] *The New York Times* (March 22, 1990).

[26] *The New York Times* (March 22, 1990).

[27] *The New York Times* (March 16, 1990).

[28] *Moving Forward: A National Agenda To Address Homelessness in 1990 and Beyond and a Status Report on Homelessness in America* (New York: the Partnership for the Homeless, 1989), 3-4; David C. Schwartz, *Combating Homelessness*, 19. Rate is for 1988–1989.

CHAPTER TWO

[1] *Moving Forward: A National Agenda to Address Homelessness in 1990 and Beyond and a Status Report on Homelessness in America* (New York: the Partnership for the Homeless, 1989).

[2] William O'Hare, "The Eight Myths of Poverty," *American Demographics* (May 1986), 25.

[3] *Ibid.*, 25.

[4] *Ibid.*, 23.

[5] Peter Marcuse, A study by James Wright and Julie Lam, *Shelterforce* (June/July 1988), 13.

[6] *Low Income Housing and Homelessness: Facts and Myths* (Washington, D.C.: Low Income Housing Information Service, Jan. 1989), Chapter Three

CHAPTER THREE

[1] *Star Ledger* (Sep. 26, 1989).

[2] *The New York Times* (Sep. 3, 1989), 51; personal correspondence (June 7, 1990).

[3] *Street News* (Nov. 1989). By June 1992 over 4 million copies were sold earning the homeless vendors $3 million.

[4] *Time* (Feb. 26, 1990).

[5] *Homewords* (Washington, D.C.: Homelessness Information Exchange, Jan. 1990).

CHAPTER FOUR

[1] Dag Hammerskjold. *Markings.*

CHAPTER FIVE

[1] *Sanhedrin* 27 (BT). References to the Babylonian Talmud will have a (BT) next to them for easier identification.

[2] *The New York Times Magazine* (Feb. 18, 1990).

[3] *The New York Times* (Feb. 14, 1990).

[4] Wayne King, "Our Towns," *The New York Times* (Jan.-Mar. 1990).

[5] Letters to the Editor, *The New York Times* (Feb. 11, 1990).

[6] *The New York Times* (Jan. 31, 1990).

[7] Letters to the Editor, *The New York Times* (Feb. 11, 1990).

[8] *The New York Times* (May 11, 1990).

[9] Charles A. Reich, author of *The Greening of America*, as quoted in *The New York Times* (May 11, 1990).

[10] "Topics of the Times," *The New York Times* (July 8, 1990).

[11] *The New York Times* (March 27, 1990).

[12] Sarah Lyall, *The New York Times* (July 18, 1990).

[13] *The New York Times* (March 27, 1990).

[14] Conversation with Toni Reinis, California Homeless Coalition (April 5, 1990).

[15] *The Effects of Subsidized and Affordable Housing on Property Values: A Survey of Research* (California: State of California Department of Housing and Community Development, 1988), i.

[16] Nathaniel C. Nash, Testimony of Jerauld C. Kluckman, Director of Compliance Programs for the Office of Thrift Supervision, before the Senate Banking

Subcommittee on Consumer and Regulatory Affairs, *The New York Times* (May 17, 1990); Robert Guskind, "Thin Red Line" *National Journal* (Oct. 28, 1989).

17 *Homelessness and Affordable Housing: A Resource Book for Churches,* ed. James A. McDaniel (New York: United Church Board for Homeland Ministries), 53. See also *The New York Times* (March 5, 1992) and Paul Krugman, *The Age of Diminished Expectations* (Cambridge, MA: MIT Press, 1992).

CHAPTER SIX

1 The Epistle of James 2:14-17.

2 Harold Kushner, *Who Needs God?* (New York: Summit Books, 1989), 204-205.

3 *Economic History of the Jews,* ed. Nachum Gross (New York: Schocken, 1975), 68.

4 Deuteronomy 26:5.

5 *U.S. Catholic* (Feb. 1990), 28.

6 Psalm 41:1.

7 *Building on Faith: Models of Church-Sponsored Affordable Housing Programs in the Washington, D.C. Area* (Washington, D.C.: the Churches Conference on Shelter and Housing, 1989), ii.

8 "The Shalom Vision for Housing," *Building on Faith,* p. iii.

9 *Leviticus Rabba* 34:9.

10 *Sanhedrin* 4.5 (BT).

11 Genesis 1:27.

12 Deuteronomy 10:18-19.

13 Galatians 6:2.

14 Isaiah 58:5-7.

15 I John 3:17-18.

16 *Avot* 3.8.

17 *Shabbat* 127a (BT).

18 *Sefer Chasidim*

19 *The Right to a Decent Home: A Pastoral Response to the Crisis in Housing* (Washington, D.C.: United States Catholic Conference, 1975).

20 Isaiah 5:8.

21 *Choices: A Study Circle on Homelessness and Affordable Housing,* Session 1: the Housing Problem, leader's questions (Pomfret, CT: Topsfield Foundation, 1990).

22 *Housing/Shelter, A Background Paper,* revised ed. (Pittsburgh: Housing Task Force, Pittsburgh Presbytery, 1988), 15; W. Fred Graham, *The Constructive Revolutionary* (Atlanta: John Knox Press, 1978), 79, 115.

23 *Street News* (Dec. 1990).

24 *Baba Batra* 1:6, 12d (BT); *Encyclopedia Judaica,* Vol XI, col. 1379.

25 Matthew 5:47.

26 *Choices: A Study Circle on Homelessness and Affordable Housing,* Session I.

27 *Gitin* 7a (BT)

28 Mark 12:42-44.

29 *Ketubah* 50 (BT); Maimonides, *Yad. Mattenot Anniyim* 7:5.

30 *Menorat ha-Maor,* Vol. 1, 35; Maimonides, *The Commandments,* Enelow ed., Vol. 2 (London: Soncino Press, 1967), 221.

31 *Ketubah* 49b (BT); Maimonides, *Yad. Mattenot Aniyim* 7:10, quoted in *Encyclopedia Judaica,* Vol. V, col. 341.

32 *Baba Batra* 93b (BT); *Lamentations Raba* 4:4.

33 *Baba Batra* 9b (BT).

34 "Gifts to the Poor," *Mishneh Torah* 10:5.

35 *Ketubah* 67b (BT).

CHAPTER SEVEN

1 Newsletter of the Interfaith Council for the Homeless of Union County, New Jersey (June 1989).

2 Matthew 8:20; Luke 2:7; the United States Catholic Conference, *Homelessness*

and Housing: A Human Tragedy, a Moral Challenge, (Washington, D.C.: 1988), 9.

[3] Bill Doulos, speech at the Rector's Forum at All Saints Church, Los Angeles (April 2, 1989).

[4] *Atlanta Constitution* (Oct. 14, 1989).

CHAPTER EIGHT

[1] *Homewords* (Washington, D.C.: Homelessness Information Exchange, Sep. 1989).

[2] Daniel Goleman, "Shelter Life: Why It's Hard to Get Out," *The New York Times* (May 24, 1990).

[3] Michael A. Leven, *The New York Times* (August 1, 1989); *Philadelphia Inquirer* (June 11, 1989); *Springfield, Mo. News-Leader* (May 15, 1989).

[4] *The New York Times* (Feb. 22, 1990).

[5] *7 Days* (Oct. 18, 1989).

[6] *Avot* 2.16.

CHAPTER NINE

[1] *Worldwide Challenge Magazine* (Oct. 1987), 62.

[2] *Habitat World* (Dec. 1990), 16.

[3] Steven Kaplan, "Women Who Make a Difference," *Family Circle* (Feb. 20, 1990).

[4] *Ibid.*

[5] *Roundup* (April 1990), 7.

[6] Anne Keegan, *Chicago Tribune* (April 16, 1989).

[7] *Christian Century* (Nov. 5, 1986); the concluding quotation is from John 15:15.

[8] Harry Boyte, *Occasional Papers* (January 1989).

[9] David C. Schwartz and John C. Glasock, *Combating Homelessness: A Resource Book* (New Brunswick, NJ: American Affordable Housing Institute, Rutgers Univ.), 88-90.

CHAPTER TEN

[1] *Moving Forward: A National Agenda to Address Homelessness in 1990 and Beyond and a Status Report on Homelessness in America* (New York: the Partnership for the Homeless, 1989).

[2] *Network Connection* (March/April 1990), 9; David C. Schwartz and John H. Glasock, *Combating Homelessness: A Resource Book* (New Brunswick, NJ: American Affordable Housing Institute, Rutgers Univ.), 23.

[3] *Comprehensive Housing Assistance Plan* (Atlanta: State of Georgia, 1987); *Pushed Out: America's Homeless* (Washington, D.C.: National Coalition for the Homeless, 1987), 31.

[4] David C. Schwartz, *Combating Homelessness: A Resource Book,* 1, E-2, E-25-6.

[5] *A Status Report on Hunger and Homelessness in America's Cities: 1989, a 27-City Survey* (The United States Conference of Mayors, Dec. 1989), 75.

[6] *The New York Times* (Feb. 12. 1990).

[7] Craig Rennebohm and Steve Bauck, *Homelessness and Affordable Housing, A Resource Book for Churches* (New York: United Church Board for Homeland Ministries), 28.

[8] *Star-Ledger* (Oct. 7, 1989).

[9] These expectations are based on conversations with dozens of housing activists on the local, state and national levels and the recommendations of many agencies working in the field. The "Vision Statement" developed by Network, a national Catholic social justice lobby, was particularly helpful.

[10] *Homewords* (Washington, D.C.: Homelessness Information Exchange, Dec. 1989), 1.

[11] Mary E. Brooks, *A Survey of Housing Trust Funds* (Washington, D.C.: Center for Community Change, 1989).

[12] Rebecca Gallatin in *Homelessness and Affordable Housing: A Resource Book for Churches,* ed. James A. McDaniel (New York: United Church Board for Homeland Ministries), 65; Neal R. Peirce and Carol F. Steinbach, *Corrective Capitalism* (New York: Ford Foundation, 1987), 66.

[13] Neal R. Peirce, *Corrective Capitalism,* 11.

[14] *Against All Odds: The Achievements of Community-Based Development Organizations* (Washington, D.C.: National Congress for Community Economic Development, 1989), 1-10.

[15] *The New York Times* (March 11, 1990).

[16] *Choices: A Study Circle on Homelessness and Affordable Housing,* Session 3 (Pomfret, CT: Topsfield Foundation, 1990).

[17] *Time* (Dec. 17, 1990), 48. Until recently, corporate participation in poverty programs had been limited to mostly charitable gifts. The addition of the Low Income Tax Credit to the tax code of 1986 turned syndication into a sound economic investment for corporations. A limited partnership or syndication is created between a nonprofit group and the corporation. The nonprofit, acting as the general partner, controls the project. The corporation via the syndicate derives income from the tax credit and real estate depreciation. This differs from most real estate syndicates that derive their income from the cash flow of the properties, causing rents to rise. *Homewords* (Dec. 1989), 5-6.

[18] Banana Kelly is named after the curving banana-shaped block of Kelly Street in New York City, where it organized the "sweat-equity" projects in the mid-1970s in which residents rehabilitated thirteen abandoned buildings largely by themselves. *Build* is an acronym for Bronx United for Leveraging Dollars.

[19] Seven philanthropies and the Prudential Insurance Company created a coalition in 1991 known as the National Community Development Initiative. With $62.5 million in grants and loans from the eight sponsors, they expect to obtain $500 million more from banks, government agencies, investors and local foundations. Their goal: to build or restore 7,500 housing units and dozens of child care centers for low- and moderate-income families in twenty major cities. The Local Initiatives Support Corporation and the Enterprise Foundation will act as intermediaries between the eight financial sponsors and the community development corporations that are the local nonprofit groups. The local groups have "solid track records over the last two decades in transforming decaying neighborhoods through the development of housing, commercial and industrial projects." Kathleen Teltsch, *The New York Times* (March 1, 1991).

[20] Neal R. Peirce, *Corrective Capitalism*, 71.

[21] See chapter seven.

[22] *Time* (Dec. 17, 1990), 48.

[23] *New York Post* (July 6, 1989).

CHAPTER ELEVEN

[1] Alexis de Tocqueville, *Democracy in America.*

[2] Avot 1.14.

[3] Dennis Hevesi, *The New York Times* (May 21, 1990).

[4] *The Polling Media* (Jan. 30, 1989); *Time* (April 16, 1990).

[5] See pages 119–120.

[6] *Low Income Housing in America: Facts and Myths* (Washington, D.C.: Low Income Housing Information Service, Jan. 1989), 38.

CHAPTER TWELVE

[1] First Century Jewish sage.

[2] *Shelterforce*, 15.

[3] Todd Swanstrom, *The New York Times* (March 23, 1990).

A RESOURCE
DIRECTORY

◆ —————————————————————————————————— ◆

American Affordable Housing Institute
P.O. Box 118
New Brunswick, NJ 08903

California Coalition for the Homeless
1010 S. Flower Street
Los Angeles, CA 90013
213-746-7677

Center for Community Change
1000 Wisconsin Avenue, NW
Washington, DC 20007
202-342-0519

Church & Temple Housing
502 1/2 S. Main Street
Los Angeles, CA 90013
213-627-3832

City Harvest
159 W. 25 Street
10th Floor
New York, NY 10001
212-463-0456

Common Cents
500 Eighth Avenue
New York, NY 10018
212-736-6437

Community for Creative Nonviolence
425 Second Street, NW
Washington, DC 20001
202-393-4409

Community Workshop on Economic Development
100 S. Morgan Street
Chicago, IL 60607

Enterprise Foundation
505 American City Building
Columbia, MD 21044
301-964-1230

Ford Foundation
320 East 43 Street
New York, NY 10017

Friends Committee on National Legislation
245 Second Street, NE
Washington, DC 20002-5795

Habitat for Humanity
121 Habitat Street
Americus, GA 31709-3498
912-924-6935

H.E.L.P. (Housing Enterprise for the Less Privileged)
12 East 33 Street
New York, NY 10016

IMPACT
110 Maryland Avenue, NE
Washington, DC 20002
202-544-8636

Interfaith Coalition for Housing
United Methodist Church
100 Maryland Avenue, NE
Washington, DC 20002
202-488-5653

Interfaith Council for the Homeless of Union County
724 Park Avenue
Plainfield, NJ 07060
908-753-4001

Into the Streets
386 McNeal Hall
St. Paul, MN 55108-1011
612-624-4700

Legal Action Center for the Homeless
220 E. 44th Street
New York, NY 10009
212-529-4240

Local Initiatives Support Corporation
733 Third Avenue
Eighth Floor
New York, NY 10017
212-455-9800

Luther Place N Street Village
Luther Place Memorial Church
1226 Vermont Avenue, NW
Washington, DC 20005
202-667-1377

MAZON, A Jewish Response to Hunger
2940 Westwood Blvd.
Suite 7
Los Angeles, CA 90064

McAuley Institute
1320 Fenwick Lane
Silver Spring, MD 20910
301-588-8110

Metropolitan New York Coordinating Council on
  Jewish Poverty
9 Murray Street
New York, NY 10007-2296
212-267-9500

National Coalition for the Homeless
1621 Connecticut Avenue, NW
Washington, DC 20009
212-460-8112

National Congress for Economic
  Community Development
1612 K Street, NW
Suite 510
Washington, DC 20006
202-659-8411

National Interfaith Hospitality Networks
121 Morris Avenue
Summit, NJ 07901
908-273-1100

National Low Income Housing Coalition and
Low Income Housing Information Service
1012 14 Street, NW, #1200
Washington, DC 20005
202-662-1530

National Student Campaign Against Hunger
 and Homelessness
29 Temple Place
Boston, MA 02111
617-292-4823

Network, A National Catholic Social Justice Lobby
806 Rhode Island Avenue, NE
Washington, DC 20018
202-526-4070

The Partnership for the Homeless, Inc.
115 West 31 Street
New York, NY 10001
212-947-3444

Religious Action Center of Reform Judaism
2027 Masschusetts Avenue, NW
Washington, DC 20036
202-387-2800

Second Harvest
116 South Michigan Avenue
Suite 4
Chicago, IL 60603
312-263-2303

United States Catholic Conference
1312 Massachusetts Avenue, NW
Washington, DC 20005-4105
202-541-3185

United States Conference of Mayors
1620 Eye Street, NW
Washington, DC 20006
202-293-7330

Publications

Habitat World
121 Habitat Street
Americus, GA 31709-3498

Homewords, a quarterly
Homelessness Information Exchange
1830 Connecticut Avenue, NW
Washington, DC 20009
202-462-7551

Network Connection
Network, a national Catholic social justice agency
806 Rhode Island Avenue
Washington, DC, 20008

Roundup
Low Income Housing Information Service
1012 14th Street, NW
Suite 1200
Washington, DC 20005

Street News
1457 Broadway
Suite 305
New York, NY 10036
212-768-7290

INDEX

◆ ———————————————————————————— ◆